Pitching

PITCHING

The Basic Fundamentals and

Mechanics of Successful Pitching

BOB SHAW

Contemporary Books, Inc./Chicago

Published by Contemporary Books, Inc.
180 North Michigan Avenue, Chicago, Illinois 60601
Manufactured in the United States of America
Library of Congress Catalog Card Number: 80-70643
International Standard Book Number: 0-8092-5913-3

Published simultaneously in Canada by
Beaverbooks, Ltd.
150 Lesmill Road
Don Mills, Ontario M3B 2T5

Action sequence photographs by Don Weiskopf
All other photographs by John H. Wettermann

This edition published by arrangement with The Viking Press

Preface

There is a desperate need to explain proper mechanics of pitching, proved successful by many great pitchers, and this need has been recognized by only a few in baseball. In golf, for example, practically all teaching golf pros agree on the fundamentals, although their teaching methods or points of emphasis vary. In pitching, on the other hand, I have found that very few pitching coaches or baseball men agree, or even know what the fundamentals are. Therefore, the purpose of this book is to establish, explain, and prove the basic and proper mechanics of pitching.

Contents

Preface   vii

I. Introduction   3

II. Basic Concepts   8

III. How to Achieve the Downward Plane   16

    1. Stance   16
    2. Pivot Foot   19
    3. Pivot Foot and Its Relationship to the Rubber 23
    4. Moving on the Rubber   24
    5. Foot Position in Set Position   27
    6. Hand Position in Set Position   29
    7. Preliminary Motion for Windup   31
    8. Hiding the Ball   33
    9. Shoulder and Hip Rotation   33
    10. Lead Leg Action   34
    11. Rushing   36
    12. Break the Hands   37
    13. The Forward Wrist   38
    14. Lead Arm Action   41
    15. Path of Arm   42
    16. Weight on Left Side and Hip Roll   46
    17. Stride   46
    18. High Elbow   47
    19. Figure Eight   47
    20. Position of Upper Body   49
    21. Toe to Toe (Follow-Through)   51
    22. Head   52

Contents

23. *Tempo*   53
24. *Proper Footwork after Follow-Through*   54
25. *Short Arm versus Long Arm*   54

Action Photographs of Pitchers   56

  1. *Early Wynn—windup*   58
  2. *Warren Spahn—windup*   60
  3. *Juan Marichal—windup*   63
  4. *Sandy Koufax—windup*   64
  5. *Lew Burdette—windup*   66
  6. *Whitey Ford—windup*   68
  7. *Billy Pierce—windup*   71
  8. *Bob Shaw—windup*   73
  9. *Sandy Koufax—set position*   74
10. *Billy Pierce—set position*   76
11. *Bob Shaw—set position*   78

IV. Coming to Grips with the Baseball   80

  1. *Tightness of Grip*   81
  2. *Two Basic Grips*   81
  3. *What Makes a Ball Move*   83

V. The Various Pitches   84

  1. *Fast Ball*   84
  2. *Curve Ball*   86
  3. *Slider or Fast Curve Ball*   92
  4. *Slow Curve*   96
  5. *Change-Up*   96
  6. *Slip Pitch*   97
  7. *Screwball*   98
  8. *Knuckle Ball*   98
  9. *Fork Ball*   99

VI. Teaching Methods   101

VII. Teaching Aids   105

  1. *Figure Eight*   105
  2. *Broom Handle*   105
  3. *Mirror*   106
  4. *Canvas Backstop*   106
  5. *Motion Pictures*   106

6. *Indian Drill* 107
7. *Pick Up Dirt* 107
8. *Hat Trick* 107
9. *Diagrams on Wall* 107
10. *Stopwatch* 108

VIII. Mental Aspects of Pitching 109

1. *Concentration* 109
2. *Mind Power* 110
3. *Relaxation* 111
4. *Mental Attitude* 111
5. *Positive Thinking* 112
6. *Aggressiveness* 113
7. *Emotional Stability* 113
8. *Superstitions and Mannerisms* 115
9. *Butterflies in Your Stomach* 115

IX. Pitcher-Hitter Relationship 116

1. *Attitude* 116
2. *Never Give In to the Hitter* 117
3. *Spot versus Area Pitching* 118
4. *Competitive Spirit* 119

X. Strength and Flexibility 120

1. *Pre-Spring Training Program,*
   or Winter Program 122
2. *Misconceptions That Still Exist Today* 139

XI. The One, Two, Three of Pitching 142

XII. Who's Covering for the Double Play? 144

XIII. Pick-Off Plays 146

1. *Runner on First* 146
2. *How to Stop the Fast Runner* 147
3. *Pick-Off Play at First*
   with Runners on First and Second 148
4. *Pick-Off at Second* 149
5. *Pick-Off at Third* 150
6. *Pick-Off at First by the Left-Handed Pitcher* 151
7. *Pick-Off at Second with Bases Loaded*
   or Runners on Second and Third 152

Contents

XIV. How to Execute Fielding Plays   153
  1. Defense against the Bunt Situation   153
  2. Backing Up the Bases   155

XV. Pitcher-Catcher Relationship   158

XVI. Pitcher-Umpire Relationship   163

XVII. Hitters' Weaknesses   164

XVIII. Pitching Strategy   169
  1. How to Set Up the Hitter   169
  2. Quick Pitch   173
  3. Pitching in a Bunt Situation   174
  4. Daily Program   175
  5. Starting versus Bullpen   177
  6. Suggestions to Your Manager   180

XIX. Bunting, Sliding, and Running   183
  1. Bunting   183
  2. Sliding   184
  3. Running   185
  4. The Delayed Steal   186

XX. Equipment and Care   188
  1. Selecting a Glove   188
  2. Shoes   189
  3. Hat   189
  4. Sweatshirt   189
  5. Supporter and Cup   189
  6. Sanitary Stockings   189
  7. Care of the Arm   191

XXI. Recovery from Injury   193

XXII. Diet and the Athlete   195
  1. Breakfast   196
  2. Lunch   197
  3. Dinner   197

XXIII. Ingredients You Must Have to Be a Success   199

Afterword   201

Index   203

Pitching

1 / Introduction

In professional sports today it is essential that the athlete obtain and maintain a high degree of skill, as well as physical and mental fitness. In baseball the trial-and-error method that still prevails takes a great deal of time and usually produces bad habits and incorrect techniques, which retard the individual's progress and shorten his career.

The statement so often made about a young pitcher, "Don't fool with him, let him develop naturally," is wrong. You cannot leave a young pitcher alone. In any sport, a beginner must learn the correct mechanics and fundamentals if he wants to reach the height of his own ability. The easy way, or natural way, is not necessarily correct. Developing pitching success and maintaining it is not a hit-or-miss proposition. It requires knowledge and the correct use of fundamentals.

The old saying, "Take a lesson from a pro," is all right, but remember there are all kinds of "pros." I have selected a number of pitchers, past and present, who were and are the best in their profession. Why? Because they have maintained themselves over a long period of time (ten years or more), have compiled enviable records, and are known in the profession as dependable pitchers, day in and day out, year after year. I am fortunate to have roomed with Early Wynn and Warren Spahn, two outstanding pitchers. Both are members of the Hall of Fame, and both lasted twenty or more years in the big leagues. Through conversations with them I know they both agree in substance on what the basic mechanics of pitching are. It is because they threw correctly that they both lasted a long time and had excellent control. When I use the word "success," I mean success that has been sustained for ten or more years in the major leagues.

I became very curious as to why these "greats" lasted so long in the highly competitive sport of baseball. After reading most of the available books and periodicals on pitching, after marathon talks with coaches, managers, and fellow players, and after constant research in my own pitching, I know I have found the reason.

There is a basic pattern that great pitchers have used, whether they knew it or not. Their styles may be different, but not their mechanics. (Yes, there is always an exception to every rule, but we are not concerned with the exception here.)

My first concrete experience with the basic mechanics of pitching was when I was traded by Detroit to the Chicago White Sox. I would like to give credit to Al Lopez and Ray Berres of the White Sox for my introduction into the wonderful world of mechanics. I started in organized baseball in 1953 and had never won more than ten games in any one season. After I joined the White Sox in 1958, with good coaching, hours of practice, and a good defensive team behind me, one year later I was able to compile a record of 18–6, which was the best winning percentage in the American League. I was third in the league with an ERA of 2.69, had the second lowest number of walks per nine innings, and came in third in the Cy Young Award balloting. I mention these figures only to illustrate a point: In less than a year I was able to reach my individual potential through the proper mechanics. I believe you can do the same.

I can name many other pitchers who, before going to Chicago, had been only mediocre but who later compiled outstanding records with the White Sox. Chicago has had great pitching year in and year out, and much credit should go to Ray Berres, the club's fine pitching coach for many years.

Proper mechanics and control are one and the same thing. The overused statement about a pitcher, "He will gain control as he gains experience," is generally made because the coach or manager doesn't really know the correct mechanics of pitching or hasn't the ability to impart this essential information to others.

If you expect me to tell you an easy way or give you some mystic knowledge that will make you a good pitcher, put the book down now and go your merry way with the trial-and-error method. Only by intensive study and hours of practice under the watchful eye of someone who knows the fundamentals, will you start on the road to permanent success. It is up to you to combine an understanding of these fundamentals with constant practice to perfect your co-ordination, rhythm, and pitching form. When this is accomplished, you will be ready to become an outstanding pitcher.

I have found that there are two main reasons why most pitchers fail. First, many have the attitude: "I have done outstandingly well in my league—why change?" Second, few have the determination to spend time on re-educating their muscles. Old habits are hard to change, and in learning something new there is almost always a temporary setback. But no matter how little skill you have, if you work hard and try to improve daily, you are bound to become more skillful—maybe not at first, but eventually. Don't discourage easily.

Anyone who has followed professional baseball knows of cases where a big bonus has been the start of complacency, the forerunner to taking the easy way out, falling back on the bankroll rather than continuing to fight on to reach a goal. Sometimes the mere signing of a "big league" contract gives a man an exaggerated opinion of his ability and starts the dry rot of overconfidence.

As a minor-league pitching coach for the Oakland Athletics and Los Angeles Dodgers, I found that many pitchers, especially in the lower minor leagues, didn't want to try new things even though they knew they were correct and would eventually help them. They were afraid they might be released if they looked bad. They knew the manager was primarily interested in winning. I say that you should not delay one day or one hour in trying to improve, no matter what the consequences! Make the corrections necessary to become a complete pitcher. Only by doing this can you reach the major leagues. Don't let insignificant reasons, which may seem important now, keep you from your ultimate goal.

Let me repeat, you will probably go backward for a while whenever you try something new, but if you know it will make you a better pitcher, by all means stay with it. I don't mean to downgrade minor-league managers, but as a pitcher you will get very little assistance and knowledge from the majority of them, because very few managers have been pitchers and their knowledge is limited. If the manager is sincerely interested in developing pitchers, he will permit and have patience during the experimental period, which in the long run will produce a winning pitcher.

There is no easy road to becoming a pitcher. There

is a road of self-denial, hard work, constant practice, ambition to improve, and an insatiable desire to do everything possible to become the best. This book is for the Little Leaguer whose coach or dad wants him to build on a sound foundation, for the high-school or college player who wants to stay on the road to the big leagues, for the pro who wants to keep collecting that "pot of gold" for a long time, and for the professional manager or coach who would like to teach specifics and not generalities.

My knowledge of these fundamentals has been developed from twenty years of professional pitching and coaching, much study, and many hours of observation of slow-motion films. My thanks go to Lew Fonseca, Director of the Motion Picture Division of the American and National Leagues of Professional Baseball Clubs, for allowing me to use various educational films and to study the many films he has on file.

II / Basic Concepts

The key to pitching success lies in the pitcher's ability to throw the ball on a *downward plane*. This means that the ball follows a downward trajectory from the point of release to home plate. The release point is approximately at the ear, as pictures taken by the latest cameras prove (P-1, Bob Buhl). The greater the angle downward, the greater the advantage to the pitcher (I-1).

Pitching on a downward plane means that the ball is moving in two planes, forward and down. Generally speaking, the batter swings the bat parallel to the ground—in a single plane. If you throw sidearm, the fast ball breaks in, but on the same plane as the bat. Likewise, the curve ball from a right-handed sidearm pitcher breaks out to a right-handed hitter, but still remains at the same level as the bat. The percentages over a period of time show that the hitter hits the ball squarely more often off sidearm pitching (I-2). I must mention that Little Leaguers as well as high-minor-league pitchers have had outstanding records throwing from the side, mainly because the inexperienced hitters or hitters with little intestinal fortitude have yielded to the pitcher. This is not the rule in the big leagues. It is sad to see a young minor-leaguer with outstanding stuff find pitching difficult in

8

I-1

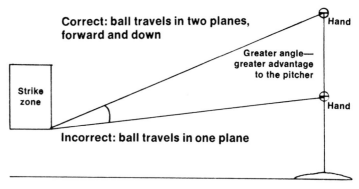

Correct: ball travels in two planes, forward and down

Hand

Greater angle— greater advantage to the pitcher

Strike zone

Hand

Incorrect: ball travels in one plane

The Downward Plane

P-2A

P-2B

I-2

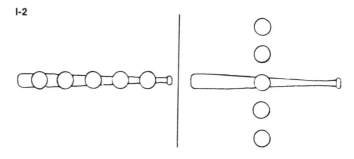

One plane: Incorrect. Bat can hit all five balls when the ball travels on a horizontal plane.

Two planes: Correct. Bat can hit only one ball if the ball moves on a vertical plane.

the big leagues. He doesn't understand why he isn't a winning pitcher.

The farther the hand goes away from the head at the point of release, the less mechanical advantage you have (P-2A—incorrect; P-2B—correct). How many sidearm pitchers are now pitching in the big leagues? Practically none. Why? Because the strain put on the shoulder and elbow is too much for muscle, ligament, and tendon structure to withstand. Ewell Blackwell, one of the greatest sidearm pitchers in modern times, compiled a fabulous record over a short period, but his arm was unable to withstand the rigors of everyday pitching. Using proper mechanics, a pitcher will undergo less strain, will have a longer career, and will bounce back more quickly, with less stiffness and soreness between pitching assignments. (Don Drysdale is an example of a pitcher who went from sidearm to a more overhand, three-quarter-arm delivery and became a consistent winner.)

Keep your lead shoulder closed. If you open it too quickly, you will lose the mechanical advantage and cause yourself much strain (I-3A—correct; I-3B—incorrect).

The elbow *must* be up, at shoulder level or above. If you pitch with a dropped elbow, your hand will be traveling almost parallel to the ground and you cannot pitch on a downward plane. The pitching coaches' command, "Get on top of the ball," is a meaningless cliché. You will have a tendency to be on an upward plane going into the release area if you throw with a dropped elbow. The ball will not move as well, it will have less velocity, an inferior flat curve will result, and your pitches will tend to come in high (P-3A—incorrect; P-3B—correct).

From the moment you begin your arm motion until its completion, your arm will draw a circle in the air, with your shoulder as the center point. The

P-3A

P-3B

10

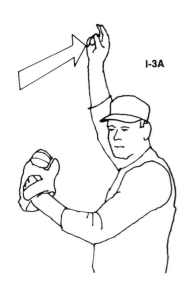

I-3A

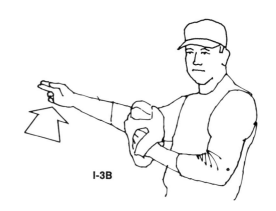

I-3B

P-4A

P-4B

P-5A

P-5B

longer the arm, or the higher you raise the elbow, the larger will be the circle. If you throw with a dropped elbow, the circle will be smaller (I-4). The larger the circle, the more momentum your arm will have when you go into the release area. This *hand speed* gives your fast ball its velocity and movement and your curve ball its sharp break. Remember, when you raise your elbow, you also increase the downward plane (P-4A, Sandy Koufax; P-4B, Juan Marichal).

It is of the greatest importance that you keep your weight on the back leg while the pitching arm swings down, back, and up. This gives the arm a chance to catch up to the body and will allow you to throw the ball on a downward plane. If you rush, the weight goes forward ahead of the arm, the elbow does not have a chance to get up, and you lose hand speed. Keep the weight back until after the arm is up; then

P-6A

P-6B

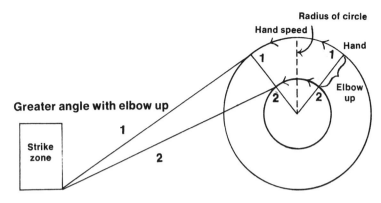

Hand Speed

In 1 and 2 elbow has traveled same distance, but hand in 1 has traveled almost twice as far as hand in 2. Hand speed gives you greater velocity. With the elbow up (1) the curve ball can be thrown harder. The ball leaves the hand on a sharper downward plane. The angle of break at home plate will be farther away from the plane of the bat. Remember that when you raise your elbow you increase the radius of the circle, which in turn gives you greater hand speed.

drive forward (P-5A—incorrect, rushing; P-5B—correct).

Break all pitches down. There are two correct deliveries, overhand and three-quarter, both of which are made with the elbow up. (We will not discuss sidearm delivery here, although in later stages of development there are instances when an occasional sidearm pitch is useful.) The overhand pitcher can make the fast ball rise: the ball will move up, out of the plane of the bat. And his curve ball will break down, away from the plane of the bat. The three-quarter sinker-ball pitcher should make the fast ball, curve, and slider move down, not over or parallel to the plane of the bat. (There is one exception on the slider for a right-handed pitcher when he is pitching to a left-handed hitter, which is discussed later.) Never forget this: *Break all pitches down.*

If you pitch on a downward plane you will have better control. Control is being able to move the ball in and out, up and down, but primarily being able to keep the ball *down* consistently. Why? The hitting area or "sweet spot" of the bat is approximately eight inches. When the hitter extends the bat over the plate shoulder-high, he can cover a pitch way outside, but as he drops his hands toward the ground, the end of the bat moves away from the outside perpendicular line and comes toward the feet, so the hitting area is reduced (P-6A, B).

With the elbow and shoulder in the proper position, breaking the ball down on the plate rather than over and off the plate, the pitcher can achieve more strikes. *Pitch from one release point, and your control will improve rapidly.*

A low ball is also harder for the hitter's eyes to focus on. It is most difficult for the eye muscles to respond quickly enough so that the eyes move to the side and down. "Watch the ball hit the bat" is a well-meaning instruction intended to help keep the hitter's head still, but it is practically impossible to follow. With a ball moving rapidly toward the hitter, his eyes cannot move laterally fast enough and focus at the point of contact. Pictures have shown that his eyes focus anywhere from two to six feet in front of the contact point (P-7A, Tommy Davis; P-7B, Pete Rose; P-7C, Maury Wills; P-7D, Tony Oliva). It is easier for the hitter to follow a high pitch because his eyes move laterally for a short distance, not to the right and down as on the low pitch. The curve ball is harder to hit than the fast ball because it changes direction more drastically, and the hitter must judge from experience where it will end up.

Keeping the ball down consistently generally means the difference between success and failure. Remember, there are four infielders plus yourself, and more ground balls are hit off the low ball. The home run is hit more often off the high ball.

I would like to make some comments before we get to the next chapter.

P-7A

P-7B

14

Temporary success can be cruel because it g
you false confidence. Real pitching success co
only when you are able to give top performance
over a long period of time. If you throw with the
correct mechanics, you will be able to pitch successfully for many years because you will have better
control and better movement on all pitches, and there
will be no excess strain on your arm or body.

Typically, the hard-throwing youngster pitches
successfully even though he is throwing mechanically wrong. He is young and strong, and the elas-
ticity in his muscles often temporarily postpones
the disaster that lies ahead—injury. He may wonder
why his control isn't improving. People probably
say, "He will develop control as he matures and
gains experience." But it seldom comes. Or a
pitcher may be very effective and then for some
reason lose his effectiveness or seem always to make
a mistake at the wrong time, so he doesn't win consistently, even though everyone says, "He's got a
great arm."

In this situation the pitcher gets the usual advice:
"You're making too many bad pitches. . . . Get on
top of the ball, follow through, shorten your stride,
bend your back." But he has already heard these
generalizations many times before. They are well-
meaning but unfortunately rarely solve the problem.

Of course anyone can see that the end result is
poor. Something has been done wrong to produce
this poor result. This book will show you specifically
what you have done wrong, rather than making
general statements.

For some pitchers it may be too late. But if you
are willing to try these basic mechanics and have
perseverance and dedication, you are at the thresh-
old of a new experience: *being able to get hitters
out consistently over a long span of time.*

P-7C

P-7D

15

III / How to Achieve the Downward Plane

Pitching a baseball is a skill that requires proper mechanics and coordination of all parts of the body into a rhythm that creates the most efficient delivery with maximum power and minimum stress and strain on the arm and body. This chapter deals with the specific mechanics necessary to put the body and arm in the proper position to pitch on a downward plane.

Let me repeat, there are exceptions to every rule. Some outstanding pitchers may not do what is suggested in this book. However, everything you read from here on is intended to make it easier for you to achieve the downward plane, reduce the margin of error, and ensure a long career.

The instructions in this book are for right-handed pitchers, but the principles are the same for left-handers. Simply reverse the instructions for left-handed pitchers.

1. Stance

A phrase often used about a business career is "Start at the bottom and work up." The same is true in pitching. Begin by getting your stance right. Stand straight up. A right-hander stands with the right foot forward, left foot back, the right foot in contact with the rubber. Feet are comfortably spread; weight is equally balanced on both feet. The throwing hand rests comfortably to the back and side of the right thigh; the glove hand rests comfortably against the left thigh.

Many pitchers hunch over, putting the glove hand on the knee. This position is not advisable because it makes the neck muscles taut and the arm has to support the weight of the upper body. It is harder to concentrate when parts of the body are under tension. It is also harder from this position to look around and check the wind or where your fielders may have moved to play the hitter. And it is easier to breathe in an upright position. Try it and see (P-8A—incorrect; P-8B—correct).

The stance should be square to home plate. Standing in a cater-cornered position is bad because the chain reaction it sets up increases the margin of error. The reason pitchers get the habit of standing this way is that it is easier to pivot in front of the rubber and thus provides a lazy way to get started. This stance is taught by a number of pitching coaches, but in my opinion it is a serious mistake. When you are square to home plate and you step back with the left foot and then start forward as you rotate into the pitch, your head has remained on the target. It has moved back and then forward, but it has not moved to the left or right of home plate. The body movement is directly toward home plate, as it should be. The cater-cornered position is bad because when you step back to the left and then transfer the weight forward, your head moves sideways from left to right, off the target. I call this incorrect movement "pitching around a corner." Also, you have a greater tendency to throw across the body because the weight is moving to the right of the target. Throwing across the body will affect your control. You will find that it is difficult to pinpoint pitches on the outside portion of

P-8A

P-8B

17

P-10A

P-9A

P-10B

P-9B

P-11

the plate consistently. Your margin of error is increased (P-9A—incorrect; P-9B—correct).

The reason you shouldn't throw across the body is that you will lock your hips. If you lock your hips, it will be difficult to follow through correctly (P-10A—incorrect; P-10B—correct).

Here's a tip: Stand with your toes pointing out slightly. This will do two things. The right toe pointed out will make it easier to rotate into the pitch. And with the toes pointed out you will want to rotate the upper part of the body rather than move forward, which would cause you to rush (P-11). *Rushing is the cardinal sin in pitching, and you will fight it as long as you pitch.*

There is an exception to the rule. An overhand pitcher who kicks his leg in front high—for example, Marichal or Spahn—stops the weight from moving to the right. Therefore he can successfully start with his hips slightly turned instead of square to home plate.

2. Pivot Foot

After you pivot, the pivot foot should be parallel to the rubber or perpendicular to home plate.

There are two ways to pitch off the rubber: partially on top of the rubber, and in front of the rubber (P-12A, B). In the big leagues pitchers are probably evenly divided between the two methods. I personally like the first method, keeping your foot partially on the rubber. As a minor-league coach the last few years, I have noticed that most young pitchers pitch in front of the rubber.

A. Partially on top: The foot is in contact with the rubber, and the angle of the foot gives you better leverage and drive—as starting blocks do for track. You always have the same feel and always

P-12A

P-12B

19

pitch from the same height and base, whereas if you pitch in front of the rubber, the dirt wears away during the course of the game. This is not so much the case in the big leagues; however, it has been my experience that the mound is not taken care of as well in the minor leagues. Sometimes they just push the dirt or sand back in front of the rubber. Clay is usually used in the big leagues, and it is harder to wear a hole in this type of mound.

I have found from experience that removing the rear spike on the right heel has made me more comfortable, especially from a set position, when pitching on top of the rubber. If you pitch in front of the rubber, removal of the middle rear spike is unnecessary (P-13).

B. In front: If you step in front of the rubber, there are other advantages. You are closer to home plate by a few inches. You can can step into the pitch and gain added momentum. Because your pivot foot is flat on the ground rather than half on the rubber, it is slightly easier to keep your weight back.

This is insignificant, but you do lose about one inch when you step in front of the rubber because you are lower and therefore decrease the angle of the downward plane. Step forward and to the right. Don't bring your pivot foot back to the left or underneath your body (P-14A, B—correct; P-14C—incorrect).

P-15A

P-15B

Branch Rickey, who had great knowledge in all phases of baseball, taught that all three front spikes should be in front of the rubber for all pitchers. This is one point that I do not agree with, whether you step in front or keep the pivot foot partially on top of the rubber. I suggest you have one of the front three spikes on the rubber. If you put all three spikes

P-16A

P-16B

PITCHING

in front of the rubber, you will feel the rubber with the instep of the foot rather than the ball of the foot when you step back—which I feel is incorrect. I have also noticed some pitchers lose their balance when they step back if the weight goes to the instep (P-15A —incorrect; P-15B—correct). When you step back with your left foot, keep the ball of your right foot in contact with the rubber.

I suggest you try both ways and see which is most comfortable or gives you the best results.

I-5

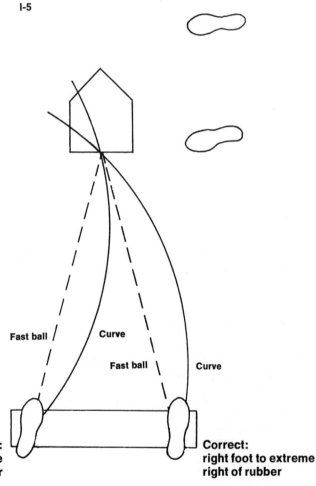

Fast ball Curve

Fast ball Curve

Incorrect:
right foot to extreme
left of rubber

Correct:
right foot to extreme
right of rubber

3. Pivot Foot and Its Relationship to the Rubber

The proper stance on the rubber, for a right-hander, is with the right foot on the right side of the rubber (reverse for left-handed pitchers) (P-16A—incorrect; P-16B—correct). Keep in mind that a right-handed hitter must cover the outside portion of the plate with his bat, so he must stand reasonably close to the plate. When a right-handed pitcher delivers the ball to a right-handed hitter, the hitter has little or no angle on the flight of the ball, so it is difficult for him to judge distance and focus on the ball (I-5). (In the same way, the hardest ball for an infielder or outfielder to judge is the ball hit directly at him. If there is a slight angle in the flight of the ball, he can judge it more easily.) Also, the curve ball from a right-handed pitcher breaks away from a right-handed batter. Managers want their hitters to have the advantage, so they put left-handed hitters in to face right-handed pitchers. The hitter then is at an angle to the path of the ball, and the curve will break to him.

I have heard that a right-handed pitcher should move over to the left side of the rubber when facing a left-handed hitter. I do not recommend this because the right-handed pitcher has his arm attached to his body on the right side. There is little advantage for him in shifting to the left side of the rubber. He will not decrease the angle that much, but he can upset or lose his pitching groove by shifting his pivot foot. The idea sounds good in theory, but I have found from experience that you lose both control and your whole perspective from the mound to home plate.

Another important reason for standing to the right is that this helps prevent the pitcher from locking his hips. When your pivot foot is on the right side of the rubber and you step directly toward home plate, your

P-17A

P-17B

23

hips are open. If your pivot foot is on the left side of the rubber and you step directly toward home, your hips are locked and it will be more difficult for you to move the ball in and out (P-17A—incorrect; P-17B—correct).

Left-handed pitchers should be on the left side of the rubber for the same reason that a right-hander is on the right side of the rubber. In a set position or stretch position, the left-hander should be on the extreme left side of the rubber for the following additional reasons: When picking off a runner, the pitcher is closer to first base; the ball will get there faster because it doesn't have to travel so far. And he will have a distinct advantage in the pick-off move to first base. The left-hander should take advantage of the fact that he needn't step directly toward first. The lead foot can step halfway between first and home. When he finishes up he will not look as if he's in front of the rubber. If his left foot is on the right side of the rubber and he makes the same move, he will appear to be directly in front of the rubber (P-18A I, II, III—incorrect; P-18B I, II, III—correct).

The exception to this rule concerns pitchers who throw a screwball often. For example, Juan Marichal of the San Francisco Giants, a right-hander who uses the screwball most effectively, pitches from the left side of the rubber. Jim Brewer of the Los Angeles Dodgers, a left-handed relief specialist, throws from the right side of the rubber because his best pitch is a screwball.

4. Moving on the Rubber

Pitchers are taught, from the Little League to the big leagues, to move the pivot foot on the rubber to adjust their control. This is dead wrong. I have never understood the logic of such teaching. In every sport

24

P-18AI

P-18AII

P-18AIII

P-18BI

P-18BII

P-18BIII

P-19A

P-19B

P-19C

from kicking a football to throwing a baseball, the direction the lead foot goes is the direction intended for the path of the ball. Move the left foot, not the right foot. *Always keep the right foot stationary and go from there.*

The misguided information so often delivered to the youngster who is missing the strike zone by four inches inside is, "Move your right foot over to the left four inches." But the instructor fails to realize two things. First, let's suppose the pitcher still misses four inches on the inside; he might possibly work himself right off the rubber. And second, if he does pitch the ball over the inside corner of the plate, his development has not improved, since he cannot control his pitches by moving the ball in and out. Let's face it, the winning pitchers can move the ball in and out, and the sooner you start, the sooner you will be a winning pitcher. *The lead foot governs control.*

There are other statements I have heard too many times, and these too seem to be logical but retard the development of the pitcher: "Throw the ball over the middle of the plate and pick up the corners." "With your stuff they won't hit you." "Throw strikes." I estimate that this philosophy retards the development of most minor-league pitchers for a number of years. Generally, after a long period of trial and error, or through observation, they come to realize that pitching to the corners and not the heart of the plate is the answer to successful pitching.

I realize that coaches in the Little League, high school, and the lower minor league want their pitchers to get the ball over the plate, because a hard-throwing youngster will win if he simply puts the ball over the plate. But temporary success only leads to a false foundation in pitching, and the coach should make every pitcher realize that his success at this point is

26

only temporary. *The ability to miss the plate at times, not to throw a strike, is just as important as throwing strikes.* The ability to move the ball in and out and up and down for strikes, and also to miss the plate by inches when he wants to, will make a highly successful pitcher and consistent winner.

Experience has taught me that the best method of teaching command of the fast ball is to exaggerate the position of the catcher by moving him three or four feet to the right of home plate for three pitches, and then three or four feet to the left of home plate. The wilder a pitcher is, the farther I move the catcher away from the plate. Most coaches have the catcher sit in the middle of home plate, saying, "Throw strikes." My method forces the pitcher to make adjustments, and he learns how to compensate to make the ball go where he wants it to go.

P-20

5. Foot Position in Set Position

There are three ways for a right-hander to stand: closed (P-19A), square (P-19B), and open (P-19C). The overhand pitcher starts his delivery by dropping the back shoulder. The correct front shoulder action is up and down. Therefore the closed stance is an advantage because by simply picking up the lead leg you automatically drop the rear shoulder, which puts you in the desired position with the least amount of leg movement (P-20).

The three-quarter-arm pitcher will want to rotate his shoulders slightly from left to right, with shoulders remaining parallel to the ground. The open stance allows you to roll into the pitch, coming closer to the windup delivery and allowing you to get some momentum, and makes it easier to keep the weight back (P-21).

The square stance may be used by either the over-

P-21

27

P-22A

P-22B

P-22C

P-23A

P-23B

hand or three-quarter pitcher if he finds it suits him best.

There is flexion in the right leg in the set position. Never stand with your legs straight and stiff.

I realize that many baseball men will not recommend the open stance for a right-hander because the runner will steal when you rotate the shoulder slightly toward home plate. You will be surprised, if you give thought to it, how few good base-stealers there really are. And if the opposition is three runs down, they probably won't steal anyway. So why handicap yourself? The problem of preventing base-stealing will be taken up later.

6. Hand Position in Set Position

The hands should meet and come to a stop approximately at the belt buckle, with both palms facing your belt (P-22A). Don't stop your hands at your chest or below your belt. If you hold them high you will have excess tension in the muscles of the arms (P-22B). If your hands are too low, you have to raise them extra high to get started, which takes longer and permits the runner to get an extra jump (P-22C).

In a set position, you first lift both hands up together; then the hands break. You pick up your lead leg and your hands at the same time. This makes it easier to keep the weight on the back leg (P-23A, B). Many pitchers make the mistake of breaking the hands and starting forward at the same time. This leads to rushing. The pitcher who breaks his hands without first lifting them slightly generally fails to keep his weight back, and because he rushes he will end up throwing with a dropped elbow. Loss of velocity and high pitches will result.

P-24A

P-24B

29

P-25A

P-25B

P-26A

P-26B

P-25C

P-25D

P-26C

7. Preliminary Motion for Windup

Keep the head up, concentrating on the target. All pitchers get lazy at times and drop the head during the preliminary motion and take their eyes off the target. This is a bad habit.

There are three preliminary motions. Start with the hands together in front of your body. As the hands come up and over your head, you step back with the left foot. Then shift the weight forward as you rotate into the pitch (P-24A, B). This method is used primarily to hide the pitches. It is most difficult to detect grip, angle of the wrist, and so on, when the pitcher is using this preliminary motion. It is a compact move and has become quite popular in recent years.

The second is perhaps more relaxing and allows you to get into the "swing of the pitch." Stand erect, square to home plate, with hands at your sides and your head up. The hands swing forward in front of the body and touch, as you bend slightly at the waist. As the weight goes to the right leg, the hands break and swing back; the backs of the hands should be facing home plate. Step back as your hands swing forward and up over your head, then rotate into the pitch (P-25A, B, C, D).

The third way is the same as the second, except the hands don't touch in front of the body; they go back first, and then over your head (P-26A, B, C).

I use the expression "flailing" to describe a pitcher who begins his pumping motion with the arms swinging back and away from the body rather than close to his sides. Flailing gives you a tendency to rush with the upper part of the body. Because you have no body motion, you feel you must get started, so you go forward rather than stay back. Anything that makes it easy to rush should be avoided (P-27A—incorrect; P-27B—correct).

P-27A

P-27B

31

-28A

P-28B

P-28C

P-29A

P-29B

The hands should go back over your head naturally, unrestricted. Let them go back as far as they want. Do not stop the hands in front of the head. The arms should both come back over the head. Bringing the hands to the side of the face is wrong, because it too has a tendency to make you rush (P-28A, B—incorrect; P-28C—correct).

If the elbows are wide apart you will want to rotate rather than let the body go forward too quickly; this helps to prevent rushing (P-29A—incorrect; P-29B—correct).

Tips: Don't step back too far; don't let the upper body bend backward; use your left foot as a rocker; keep the right toe down, in contact with the rubber.

8. Hiding the Ball

There is one accepted way to hide the ball. The right hand with the ball goes into the glove and the left thumb and little finger clasp just above the right wrist. The back of the glove hand is toward the batter. The purpose of doing this is to eliminate any chance of giving away the pitch (P-30A, B).

I gave up two home runs in one game to Mickey Mantle in Kansas City, and both were off curve balls that Bobby Richardson called to Mickey because I was cocking my wrist in the glove and he could see the ball from the bench. If you hide the ball correctly, the opposition will not be able to detect your pitches.

9. Shoulder and Hip Rotation

In the preliminary motion, when the hands come back over the head and the weight moves to the right foot, the left shoulder rotates and draws a bead on home plate (P-31A). Do not let the left shoulder continue toward third base. In short, aim the lead

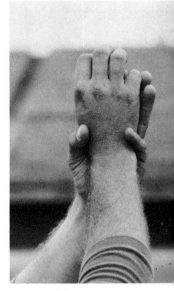

P-30A

P-30B

33

P-31A   P-31B

P-31C

PITCHING

shoulder at the target. The farther you rotate the shoulder, the greater the margin of error (P-31B). The *lead leg action* governs the shoulder rotation. Remember, not rotating enough can be worse than rotating too much (P-31C).

10. Lead Leg Action

You have started in a square position to home plate and have rotated into the pitch. The fundamental action most often performed improperly is that of the lead leg (the left leg for right-handed pitchers). The left knee should come up with the toe pointing down (P-32). If you pick the toe up, you will have a tendency to land on your heel, and you will be throwing against a stiff front leg. This makes it difficult to bend at the waist and follow through correctly. The lead leg should not swing backward past the rubber. If the leg swings backward, the upper part of the body has a tendency to go forward in a forward press, causing you to rush. Picking the leg up in front will help keep the weight back.

It should be mentioned here that if you kick your leg back, you must carry your hands back also. When you carry your hands back and break them, the path of the arm is altered in a way that I call "arm-hooking"—the arm hooks behind the body for balance. This simply increases the margin of error, reduces the chance of attaining pinpoint control, and is a major cause of elbow and shoulder injuries (P-33). The arm position is altered to the point where it is most difficult to get the elbow up to throw on a downward plane, because you have rushed.

I repeat, the leg kick is in front of the body, not in back. It will keep the weight back and allow you to swing the arm down, back, and up so that the ball will be released in a downward plane and you will eliminate one factor that causes poor control.

34

How to Achieve the Downward Plane

It should be mentioned that the three-quarter-arm pitcher can rotate his lead leg back farther than can an overhand pitcher. The reason is that an overhand pitcher drops his back shoulder, which prevents him from rotating. Overhand pitchers can lift or kick the lead leg high. Three-quarter-arm pitchers cannot give a high leg kick. For example, Warren Spahn, Juan Marichal, and Bob Feller all have high leg kicks and all were (or are) overhand pitchers. When you kick your lead leg high in front of you, the front hip must go up, and that forces the lead shoulder to go up and the back shoulder to go down. End result: you must throw overhand (I-6A).

On the other hand, a three-quarter-arm pitcher shouldn't kick his leg high but should rotate his hips, which rotates his shoulders. In this case you do not want to drop your back shoulder. This motion will enable you to bring your arm across your body from a three-quarter position (I-6B).

P-32

P-33

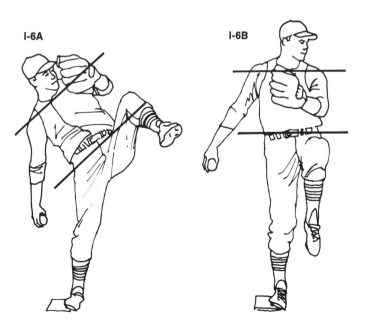

I-6A

I-6B

P-34

P-35

Do not stretch the leg out (P-34). This slows the arm action down, making it difficult to get the elbow up into the correct position, and also makes you arch your back, which is bad.

Do not flip your leg (P-35).

11. Rushing

This is the biggest culprit of them all.

Rushing occurs when the body is ahead of the arm. You lose all mechanical advantage, and the result is tremendous strain on the shoulder and arm. You lose speed and throw high pitches; the ball will not move well, and your breaking pitches will be flat and more than likely high. As I said earlier, you have a tendency to throw on an upward plane, or you compensate and drop the elbow when you rush (P-36A). It's impossible to get on top of the ball when you rush. Many pitching coaches stress driving hard with the back leg, saying, "Use the body, not just the arm." This generally does more harm than good because the pitcher thinks only of driving forward with the body and leaves the arm behind.

Yes, you do drive forward with the back leg, but first the hands have separated, the arm has swung down, back, and up, with elbow shoulder-high or higher and the weight back. *Now* you drive forward. The arm is in the proper position for delivering the ball on a downward plane (P-36B). Keep in mind that when the left foot lands the throwing arm is back and up. An analogy with hitting shows the same effect. The poor hitter allows his hands to come in to the body as he strides forward. Don't drive forward until the hands break and the arm is up.

So when we talk of rushing, we merely mean that the upper part of the body is too far ahead of the arm.

36

You will constantly hear coaches remark that "the pitcher is throwing just with his arm." They see the end result, with the pitcher standing upright, and come to this conclusion. However, what they should say is, "He tried to throw the ball with his body." The pitcher has actually rushed. In order to compensate he has no choice but to stiffen his front leg and raise his upper body to get his arm through. When he rushed he also bent his back too soon, and this too makes him lift his body back to an upright position.

Red Adams, the outstanding pitching coach of the Los Angeles Dodgers, who also believes in the importance of mechanics of delivery, best describes the movement forward of the upper part of the body—"as if you were a wall falling forward." The top of the wall topples first. "Push off" the rubber is a better expression than "drive off." We both feel that the upper part of the body, as it goes forward, pulls you off the rubber.

Other expressions used in coaching to reduce rushing are: "Try to retain your weight"; "Keep the weight on your back leg longer."

P-36A

12. Break the Hands

When you start with the proper leg kick, the weight is automatically back on the right leg and ensures good balance. This simplifies the movement and allows you to keep a constant position, so you can get into the so-called groove. In order to throw on a downward plane, you must break the hands in a definite fashion. Why? If you carry the hands back without breaking them, you have a tendency to start forward with the upper body (rushing), with the right arm still down and back behind you in the position called "arm-hooking." If you think in terms of breaking the hands quickly, then the right arm has an oppor-

P-36B

37

P-37A

P-37B

P-37C

tunity to swing down, back, and up, with the weight still back on the right leg. Now you are in a position to move forward, releasing the ball on a downward plane. Remember, if you are high with your pitches, it is most important that you break your hands quickly and keep your weight back. Your hands should move vertically to the ground, not horizontally (I-7A—correct; I-7B—incorrect).

A basic fundamental: *break your hands in the middle of your body, before you get to your belt.*

Some coaches will tell you, if you get hit hard, "Show your rear end to the hitter, rotate more. This will hide the ball and you will be more deceptive." *This is poor advice and will do more harm than good.* You will kick your leg back, carry your hands back too far, and increase the margin of error. Finding a pitching groove will be almost impossible.

Keep your hands away from your body (P-37A, P-37B—Camilo Pascual). Don't bring them in close (P-37C). An overhand pitcher can bring his hands in closer to his body than a three-quarter-arm pitcher can. Keeping your hands away from your body will help keep the lead shoulder closed longer.

13. The Forward Wrist

The proper wrist action is as follows: the hand bends forward at the wrist as you pull the throwing hand out of the glove (P-38A). This position is called "the forward wrist." Then, as the arm swings back and up, the hand bends back and then forward as you release the ball. Fly casting is the best analogy to show the correct wrist movement (I-8). When you break your hands and the throwing hand goes down and back, the palm is never up but always facing the ground (P-38B—correct; P-38C—incorrect).

38

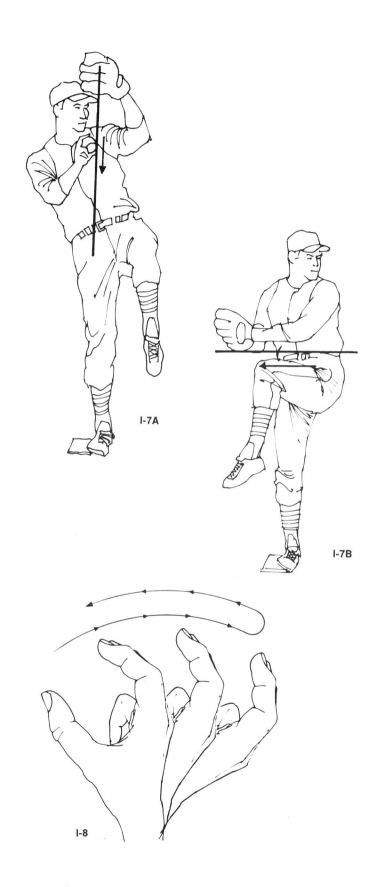

I-7A

I-7B

I-8

P-38A

P-38B

P-38C

P-39

P-40A

P-40B

P-40C

P-41A

P-41B

14. Lead Arm Action

Most of what I have heard about the lead arm action, I am convinced is wrong. When I was in high school and college I heard, "Throw the left hand at the hitter and this will add to your deception." However, I believe it hurts the pitcher in two ways. First, the right arm is going in one direction and the left arm is going in another direction (P-39). Second, if you throw the palm of the left hand at the hitter you automatically open the lead shoulder and lose mechanical advantage. In essence, you do not deceive the hitter, because the glove actually doesn't stay near the release point of the pitching hand and you put a tremendous strain on the shoulder and elbow because the timing of the pitch is broken. The correct lead arm action is as follows: The glove hand goes back with the right hand and when it comes forward the back of the hand goes toward the hitter (P-40A), or the palm faces the ground (P-40B). Never have the palm facing the batter (P-40C). If you do, you will open up the lead shoulder and lower the right elbow and arm. Correct hand position will keep the shoulder closed for maximum leverage and power with little strain on the shoulder (P-41A—incorrect; P-41B—correct). It is ideal to keep the glove hand above the elbow of your lead arm. If you drop the hand below the elbow, as many pitchers do, your left elbow will be up, which in turn forces the left shoulder up, which then makes you drop your back shoulder. End result: you make it difficult to get on top of the ball.

As the throwing hand follows through, the glove comes toward the body, palm facing chest (P-42A). Keep your elbow next to your side. This is important for two reasons: you can protect yourself faster on a ball hit back at the pitcher, and you can follow

P-42A

P-42B

P-43A   P-43B

P-43C

through more easily in this position. The left arm should not fly behind the body; don't straighten it (P-42B). This is dangerous and hinders the follow-through. If the arm is straightened it will take longer to get the glove in front of your face to protect yourself.

Thank goodness for reflexes; they will help protect you. If you play a great deal of pepper, you will quicken your reflexes; it's a great all-around conditioner.

Don't squeeze the glove hand tight. This will cause muscle tension throughout the body.

Don't open the lead shoulder too quickly. As the pitching hand moves forward, the shoulder will open up automatically. Don't consciously open the lead shoulder or you will lose mechanical advantage.

Do not tuck your glove under your arm. This too will cause you to raise the lead shoulder, and you will have to fight to get on a downward plane (P-43A—correct; P-43B, C—incorrect).

Tip: Try to bring the elbow of your lead arm *down* hard. This forces the shoulder and throwing arm into the proper position. Don't move the elbow of the lead arm to the left.

15. Path of Arm

Bottom half of circle: If you have a poor leg kick or carry your hands back, the arc of the arm will generally result in arm-hooking (see P-33 under "Lead Leg Action"). If the leg is kicked back too far, the arm must go in the opposite direction for balance. Then, when your weight goes forward, your arm is too far back and has to travel a greater distance. Most often, if you do this, you will miss inside or be high and inside. Correct lead leg action and breaking the hands in the middle of the body usually eliminate

42

P-44A

P-44B

P-44C

P-44D

arm-hooking. The correct path of the arm is as follows: *down, back,* and *up.* I describe it as a "pendulum action." This puts you in control of the ball with your elbow up as you go into the power release area. Keep your pitching hand moving and don't stop it behind your back or up on top.

Top half of circle: After the ball is released, the path of the arm should always go across the body and down. What makes a ball move, gives it spin? The movement of the hand from one extreme to the other. (Bernoulli's principle, the scientific reason why a ball changes direction while traveling through the air, is explained later.) Imagine a perpendicular line through the middle of the body to the ground. However far to the right of that line the hand goes, it must be that far to the left of the line at the end of the follow-through (P-44A, B—overhand; P-44C, D —three-quarter-arm). This is what I mean by "from one extreme to the other." If you do not go from one extreme to the other, you are quitting on the pitch, not following through properly. At the same time, the hand must go from a high point to a low point,

43

P-45AI
  P-45BI

P-45AII
  P-45BII

P-45AIII
  P-45BIII

P-46

P-47A

P-47B

not travel parallel to the ground (P-45AI, II, III—correct; P-45BI, II, III—incorrect).

Always keep the forearm perpendicular to the ground. Never let your hand move past the perpendicular toward your head (P-46). If you do, the radius of your circle will be reduced, control will be poor, and you will find it difficult to make the arm come down and across the body properly. It is difficult to throw a hard curve from this position.

Here's a tip. If you want a faster curve, simply move your hand away from your head. The closer your hand is to your head, the slower and bigger your curve ball.

Many pitchers, in learning the curve, wrap the hand too much, so that they have to bend the forearm in toward the ear. But they do not throw the fast ball from off the ear, and so this motion on the curve gives away the pitch. I recommend getting the hand up and away from the ear on all pitches.

Avoid jerking the head to the left or moving the upper part of the body to the left. Trying to throw too hard will cause you to rush, open your shoulder too soon, and jerk your head. When you try to throw to a specific spot, usually low and away, sometimes you may find yourself doing it with your head and upper body rather than with the hand. Then the ball generally goes up and in, just the opposite of what you intended (P-47A—incorrect; P-47B—correct).

Pitching is hand speed, and you can't achieve this with the body way ahead of the arm. You achieve velocity by hand speed, not by body movement.

Always reach out when throwing the ball. This increases the hand speed and allows you to maintain a groove (P-48A, B, C, Billy Pierce). You should have the feeling that the arm is accelerating in front of the body. There should be little or no feeling of movement or effort in the upper body.

Many pitchers do not bring the throwing hand

P-48A   **P-48B**

P-48C

45

P-49A

P-49B

P-49C

across the body correctly. Here is a tip. Pretend there is a perpendicular line, starting directly opposite your head, about three feet in front of you. Make sure the path of the hand crosses this line *at chest height*. Remember, if the head moves to the left, which it will slightly, the imaginary line will also move to the left. If the path of the hand is incorrect, it will cross the line at knee level, or not at all.

In the follow-through, when the hand is directly in front of you, bend at the waist. Actually, your hand pulls the upper body down. Don't bend at the waist before your hand gets to this point, or you will reduce your hand speed and impair a fluid delivery (P-49A, B, C, Camilo Pascual).

A term used by Kenny Meyers, coach and scout with the California Angels organization, describes the correct position as you follow through: "You must have a *long side*." In the correct position your arm is extended, with the right shoulder ahead of the left shoulder, and the right leg is back. Your momentum will bring the right leg up (P-50; P-49C also shows the "long side").

16. Weight on Left Side and Hip Roll

When the weight goes forward, it should be over the lead leg. Don't let it move to the right. If you roll your hips you can prevent this from happening. A good exercise is to put your right instep up on a bench and practice your follow-through. You will notice that your chest is over the lead leg and your head is to the left of your lead leg.

17. Stride

An extremely long stride is harmful because it makes it difficult to get your weight over your lead leg, and

46

your arm has a tendency to travel parallel to the ground so it is not easy to get "on top of the ball." Your stride should be straight ahead and not too long. Shorten your stride on the curve ball so you can pull down and impart better spin. The long stride may slow the arm action. The ideal is fast hand and arm action on all pitches, especially with the curve ball.

The following demonstration will show whether your stride is correct with regard to your lead foot. Do not throw across your body. Imagine a line between the toe of the pivot foot and the middle of home plate. Your lead foot should land slightly to the left of the line (I-9). However, if you step too far left you will force your lead shoulder open too soon and lose your leverage and drive forward.

P-50

18. High Elbow

As I have already said, the elbow should be at shoulder level or higher. You want to be in command of the pitch, and if the elbow is not up, you cannot pitch on a downward plane. The high elbow increases the radius of the circle, which increases the hand speed and enables the pitcher to have greater speed and a much improved curve ball. Outstanding curve-ball pitchers throw with a high elbow. The curve ball is thrown very much as if you were executing a karate chop; it is mainly hand speed, plus wrist snap, that produces the outstanding curve.

If your elbow is up, the ball will go down.

If your elbow is down, the ball will go up.

19. Figure Eight

The expression "figure eight" is used to help you visualize the synchronization of the parts of the body

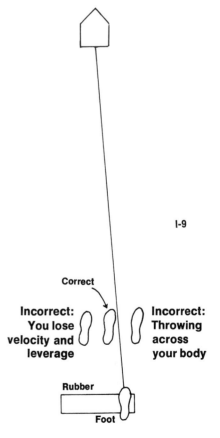

I-9

47

P-51A

P-51D

P-51B

P-51E

P-51C

P-51F

P-51G

P-51H

P-51I

involved in pitching. Stand with the left toe of your left foot pointed toward home plate, your right foot parallel to the rubber. Spread your hands about fifteen inches apart, or hold a basketball, and describe a figure eight in the air, as in the illustrations (P-51A—I). Concentrate on the up-down portion of the figure eight. Say to yourself, "Up-down," as you do the exercise. The body doesn't move very much, but the arms do.

20. Position of Upper Body

Dipping: Dipping is caused by up-and-down motion of the body because you are bending and then stiffening the back leg. Flexion in the right leg is important, but overflexion will make you bob your head so it will be difficult to concentrate on the target. There should be no up-and-down movement of the body. You should gradually lower your body as you go through your motion, but do not lower it too much (P-52A—incorrect; P-52B—correct).

Collapsing: Collapsing occurs when the upper body bends forward too much at the waist. There should be a *slight* bend at the waist, but in collapsing you are unable to get the arm up into its proper position. Consequently you start forward with the body and leave the arm behind, giving yourself very bad body alignment and poor arm position. Remember the body and the arm must work together. When you are in an upright position the arm can swing up easily. When you bend at the waist you stop the arm from going up (P-53—incorrect).

Arching: Arching the upper body back will make you tend to open your lead shoulder too soon, which will cause a slightly dropped elbow. And you know the results: loss of mechanical advantage, which means strain on the shoulder and elbow; a long re-

P-52A

P-52B

49

P-53

P-54

P-55AI

P-55AII

P-55BI

P-55BII

covery period between assignments; and a short career. You will cast the curve ball; you will quit on the pitch and find it hard to follow through, especially on the curve. Arching also makes it easier to come out "palm up" when you break your hands, which is not correct (P-54—incorrect).

Dipping, collapsing, and arching all restrict the proper action of the throwing arm. It should go down, back, and up in uninterrupted motion, once you break your hands. The upper part of the body should be in an erect position, with flexion in the legs.

21. Toe to Toe (Follow-Through)

The expression "toe to toe" describes the transfer of the weight from the right leg to the left leg, which enables the upper part of the body and right arm to follow through naturally, without any conscious effort.

If you put the weight on the ball of the right foot, there will be flexion in the right knee. This is the correct position of the right leg. In discussing lead leg action I mentioned that the toe should be pointed down. When the weight is transferred to the ball of the left foot, the left knee is bent. This is the correct position for the left leg (lead leg).

Because the lead leg is bent, the follow-through becomes automatic. If you land on the heel of the lead foot, the lead leg will tend to straighten, and you will find it difficult to bend at the waist. Therefore the follow-through will be incomplete (P-55AI, II–incorrect; P-55BI, II–correct).

If the toe of your right foot makes a long mark of more than 1½ feet on the ground, the chances are you are not pushing off with the back leg correctly. If you check, you will notice that you are probably stiffening the back leg or just not pushing off hard

P-56A

P-56B

51

P-57A

P-57B

P-57C

enough. Thinking "toe to toe" should correct this problem (P-56A—incorrect; P-56B—correct).

Think "toe to toe," and many pitching problems will disappear. A shorter stride will result, and this is beneficial. You will automatically bend your back. Remember, the arm passing in front of your body pulls the upper body down; you don't consciously bend your back.

22. Head

As in most sports, the head should be kept as still as possible, so that the eyes can focus on the target, the arm can accelerate in front of the body, and the path of the arm can come across the body correctly. A common error is to jerk the head to the left when trying to throw extra hard. The jerking of the head will cause the upper part of the body to rush and also to open up too soon. Sometimes, as I said earlier, you may try to throw to a specific spot, using your head and upper body, and the ball does just the opposite of what you want. The same thing happens when you jerk your head. The shoulder opens too soon, you release the ball too soon, and it ends up exactly where you don't want it to go.

Keep your head still, keep your weight back, and get the elbow up.

With men on base, when you are pitching from a set position, the head should move laterally, never up and down (P-57A, B—correct; P-57C—incorrect). If you move the head up and down, you make it easier for the runner to get a jump on you. He knows you must lift your head to throw home. Some pitchers move their heads real quick to deceive the runner. I believe this is wrong because it is impossible to concentrate on the target while you move your head vigorously.

52

In a set position, be sure you pick up the target (the catcher's glove) before you start your delivery home. Doing this will help your control.

To keep from moving your head or lead shoulder too far left and to help bring your arm across your body correctly, think in terms of moving your head or chin forward, directly at home plate. After I learned this idea from Red Adams of the Dodgers, I was amazed at how it helped many pitchers' control.

23. Tempo

Some people use the word "timing," or "coordination," or "rhythm." I prefer the expression "tempo." I believe there is an analogy between the backswing in golf and the backswing in pitching. In golf you are constantly told, "Take it back low and slow." The object is to build up momentum as you go into the contact area in golf and the object is the same as you go into the release area in pitching. In pitching it is most important that you go slowly and smoothly as you rotate, break the hands properly, and let the arm swing down, back, and up, with the weight back. Now you are ready to explode into the release area, and release the ball on a downward plane.

All outstanding pitchers have a slow and easy tempo but exert a tremendous amount of effort going into the release area. This is where you need maximum hand speed (I-10).

The pitcher who rushes through the preliminary

I-10

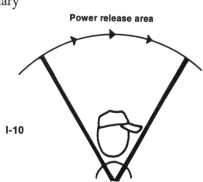

Power release area

Going into release area,
maximum effort should be applied

P-58A

P-58B

P-58C

motions is working too hard. It takes time to get the arm in the proper position. Hurrying is not the answer. On the other hand, if you go too slowly you may not be able to pick up your momentum.

Try pausing at the top of your delivery, as your hands pass over your head during your preliminary motion. This will slow you down and reduce rushing.

24. Proper Footwork after Follow-Through

As you follow through, after releasing the ball, all your weight is over your lead leg. Because you have come off the rubber with such force, you can't just put your right foot down and be in a position to field. The correct footwork is as follows: Move forward with right-left footwork to bring you square to home plate (P-58A, B, C).

Some pitchers cross over the lead leg. It is not a good thing to do, but the important thing is to put maximum effort into the pitch. If you do cross over your lead leg, which will cause you to be on the left side of the mound as you look into home plate, simply bring your left foot back around to bring you square to home plate (P-59A, B, C).

25. Short Arm versus Long Arm

I have tried to figure a way of believing that a short-arm pitcher is throwing correctly, that this is his style. But the more I study, the more I realize that the short-arm pitcher is throwing mechanically wrong in every department. The illustration I-4, showing "the circle," in the chapter "Basic Concepts" should prove that the short-arm pitcher loses the mechanical advantage of hand speed and the downward plane.

The short-arm pitcher does many of the following wrong things: He stands cater-cornered. He has a

54

tendency to bring the hands to the side of his face. He kicks his lead leg back too far, which causes an over-rotation of the shoulder past the target, arm-hooking, and rushing. Because the body is ahead of the arm, he will be on an upward plane going into the release area, so in order to compensate he drops the elbow. This has made him a short-arm pitcher. The end result: poor control, ineffective curve and slider, strain on elbow and shoulder—a pitcher who looks good today, bad tomorrow. He has no consistency, and probably a career cut short by injury.

I have observed that some short-arm pitchers end up as relief pitchers. To be a starter you should have command of three different pitches plus the stamina to go nine innings.

The short-armer will have a difficult time mastering three good pitches and, because he throws mechanically incorrectly, he will find it difficult to go nine innings.

Having one good pitch, however, will allow him to get by if he faces the same hitter only once or twice in a ball game.

P-59A

P-59B

P-59C

55

Action Photographs of Pitchers

The following pictures illustrate the basic fundamentals covered so far in this book. You will notice that each pitcher has a distinct style of his own, but each follows the basic fundamentals I have outlined:

All pitchers start their preliminary motion in one of the three ways recommended in this book.

They stand square to home plate.

The hands drop over the head during the preliminary motion.

The pivot foot is parallel to the rubber, half on and half in front of rubber.

Right-handers stand on the right side, left-handers on the left side of the rubber. The one exception is Marichal, and he throws the screwball.

The lead leg action is in *front* of the body. Some overhand pitchers have a high leg kick; three-quarter-arm pitchers have a lower leg kick.

Hands break in the middle of the body. The hands move vertically when they come back over the head.

Shoulders and hips rotate only far enough so that shoulder points at home plate.

In lead arm action, hands don't go in opposite directions.

Upper body is upright—no collapsing or arching of waist. (Marichal arches his back slightly.)

56

The path of the arm is down, back, and up (pendulum action—no arm-hooking).

"Forward wrist."

Weight is back—no rushing. The back leg is slightly bent, and the pitcher lands on a bent lead leg.

The elbow is high to deliver ball on a downward plane.

The hand is away from the head, with forearm at least perpendicular to the ground. In three-quarter-arm delivery the hand is even farther away from the head. Notice none of these pitchers throws side-arm.

The stride is straight; you will observe none of the pitchers illustrated throws across his body or locks his hips.

The ball leaves the hand approximately level with the ear.

The upper body is tilted slightly forward at release point. The arm extends in front, and this action pulls the upper body down. There is no definite break in the waist until the arm is in front of the body.

All pitchers follow through with the throwing arm, past the lead leg, maintaining the groove.

1. Early Wynn WINDUP

Stands square to home plate (1-1), toes slightly out to help reduce rushing (1-1). Hands drop over head (1-2). Shoulders and hips rotate no farther than home plate (1-5). Hands move vertically (1-4, 5, 6). Breaks his hands in the middle of his body (1-6). Path of arm is down, back, and up—no arm-hooking (1-7—10). Lead leg action is in front of body—he does not kick leg behind the rubber (1-6). He does not give an exaggerated high leg kick (1-6) because he throws from a three-quarter-arm delivery (notice his forearm is not quite perpendicular) (1-12). Notice how the correct mechanics keep his weight back—rushing (1-1—9). Lead leg lands with throwing arm back and up (1-10). Notice upper body is upright with throwing arm going into release area (1-11, 12). Arm pulls upper body down (1-14). A great competitor.

1-4   1-5   1-6

1-10   1-11   1-12

1-1   1-7   1-2   1-8   1-3   1-9

1-13   1-14   1-15

2. Warren Spahn WINDUP

Warren swung his hands back high during his preliminary motion, which was quite picturesque. Pictures do not show it, but he was slightly turned, not completely square to home plate, but remember he had a high leg kick, slightly toward home plate (2-4) and was an overhand pitcher (2-15), which kept his weight back (2-1—8). Foot is parallel to rubber. Rotation of hips and shoulders goes no farther than home plate (2-6). Hands break in the middle of his body (2-4). Back of glove is to home plate and above elbow (2-9). He keeps lead shoulder closed as long as possible by correct lead arm action, which is why he lasted so long—no strain on elbow and shoulder (2-1—12). Palm of glove is to chest (2-14—18). Glove is in a good position to defend himself (2-18). He could finish a game as well as anybody.

2-4

2-5

2-6

2-10

2-11

2-12

2-1   2-7   2-2   2-8   2-3   2-9

2-13   2-14   2-15

16   **3-1**   **2-17**   **3-2**   **2-18**   **3-3**

3-7   **3-8**   **3-9**

3. Juan Marichal WINDUP

Juan, like Spahn, is not completely square to home plate, but remember he too has an exaggerated high leg kick and is an overhand pitcher. This holds the weight back (3-7). Juan pitches off the opposite side of the rubber, but remember he throws a screwball. Foot is parallel to rubber (3-6). Hands break over lead leg in the middle of the body (3-6). Path of arm shows pendulum action (3-7–10). Notice in pictures (3-7, 8) that his palm is facing the ground, not up. He has correct lead arm action —palm not facing hitter and glove hand level with elbow (3-8). Elbow is high, arm perpendicular to ground (3-13). Weight is on left side and throwing arm past thigh, showing "long side" (3-16, 17). The most consistent pitcher I have seen pitch over a full season.

3-4

3-5

3-6

3-10

3-11

3-12

3-13   **3-14**   **3-15**

4. Sandy Koufax WINDUP

Stands square to home plate (4-1), hands behind head (4-2). Excellent lead leg
action; he doesn't kick it back, but slightly toward home (4-3, 4). He has a fairly
high leg kick (4-4) and he too is an overhand pitcher (4-10) and keeps his weight
back (4-1—6). Breaks hands in the middle of his body (4-4). Lead arm action is
correct, arms not going in opposite directions. Glove hand goes down, back, and up
(4-4—8). Body is upright at release point (4-10). Another example of the high elbow
—arm is completely extended upward, showing increased radius of circle (4-11),
which gave him such a great fast ball and curve. Observe a good example of
"forward wrist" (4-5, 6). Watch arm pull upper body down (4-12—14). Sandy
doesn't rotate any farther than home plate (4-4). I have mentioned that the back
shoulder will drop for an overhand pitcher who kicks his leg high (4-5). Had great
mechanics and great stuff.

4   **4-5**   **4-6**

3-16   4-1   3-17   4-2   4-3

4-7   4-8   4-9

4-10   **4-11**   **4-12**

5. Lew Burdette WINDUP

Stands square to home plate (5-1). Hands drop over head (5-3). Foot is parallel to rubber with pivot foot half on top of rubber. Notice rear leg is bent and he lands on a bent lead leg. Hands break in the middle of his body (5-4). Observe there is no over-rotation (5-4). Body is upright going into release area (5-5). Throwing arm pulls upper body down. He does keep glove arm straight, which is not recommended. Lew got the most out of his ability.

5-1   **5-2**   **5-3**

4-13

4-14

5-4

5-5

5-6

6. Whitey Ford WINDUP

Stands square to home plate. Correct preliminary motion—backs of hands are to home plate and close to sides (6-1). Toes are slightly out (6-1). Hands drop over head (6-4). Hands come back over head vertically (6-5—8) and break in the middle of the body (6-8). He doesn't have a high leg kick because he throws from a three-quarter-arm delivery (6-15). Notice shoulder and hip do not move up and down but remain nearly parallel with the ground (6-7—10). Because he throws three-quarter-arm he can kick his leg back farther than an overhand pitcher, which he does (6-8). These pictures were taken from above the ground; Whitey has his elbow high (6-15). Pitching hand catches up to elbow in just a few frames (6-14—16). You can see where ball leaves hand (6-16). He is in correct position to field ball (6-18). A great clutch pitcher.

6-4   6-5   6-6

6-10   6-11   6-12

6-1   6-7   6-2   6-8   6-3   6-9

6-13   6-14   6-15

6-16   7-1   6-17   7-2   6-18   7-3

7-7   7-8   7-9

7. Billy Pierce WINDUP

Stands square to home plate (7-1). At least one spike is on top of rubber (7-2). Notice ball of pivot foot in contact with rubber (7-2). Steps in front of rubber (7-4). Hands are over head (7-3). Breaks hands quickly in middle of body (7-6). Lead leg action is correct, in front of body, not back (7-5). Rear leg is bent, and he lands on bent lead leg. Notice lead foot lands on ball of foot, knee bent, throwing hand back with lead shoulder closed in a strong position (7-8). Palm is down (7-7). Notice great lead arm action (7-7). Rear shoulder is down sufficiently to make him an overhand pitcher (7-11). Elbow is up (7-10). Ball has traveled a couple of feet and wrist has flipped forward slightly in front of ear (7-11). Arm is extended in front of body (7-12). Observe path of arm by thigh to complete perfect follow-through. It was a pleasure to watch him pitch with such a smooth delivery.

7-4   7-5   7-6

7-10   7-11   7-12

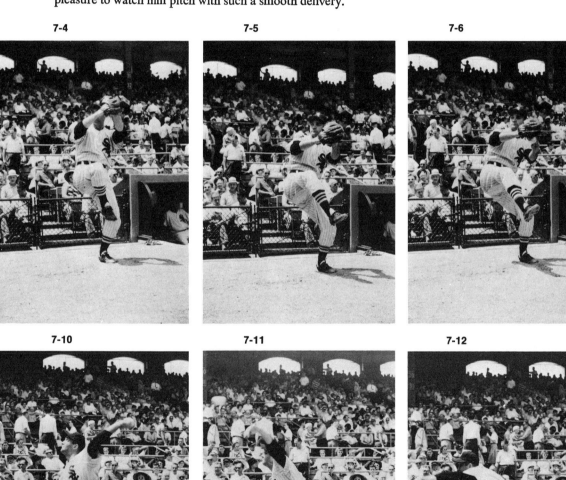

7-13

8-1

7-14

8-2

7-15

8-3

8-7

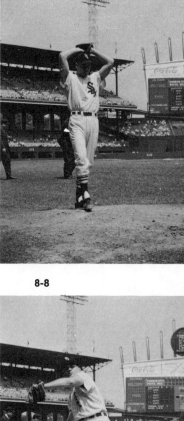

8-8

8-9

8. Bob Shaw WINDUP

The reason I included myself with such great pitchers is that I feel I can demonstrate the proper fundamentals, which were taught to me by Ray Berres. These pictures were taken in 1959. One year before, you would not have recognized me as the pitcher in the photos. This should prove that with proper coaching, correct mechanics, and hard work, *you* can become a winning pitcher.

8-4

8-5

8-6

8-10

8-11

8-12

8-13   8-14   8-15

9. Sandy Koufax SET POSITION

Foot is on left side of rubber (9-1). Closed stance (9-1)—remember I said most overhanded pitchers use a closed stance. Billy Pierce also uses a closed stance, as did Warren Spahn. (Both are overhand pitchers.) Hands are belt-high (9-1). Lead leg action is correct (9-3). He moves hands up slightly and away from body (9-3). Left knee is bent slightly (9-2). Path of arm is down, back, and up (9-4—8). "Forward wrist" (9-5, 6). Elbow is up (9-11). Arm is perpendicular to ground (9-11). Path of arm is down and across body in perfect follow-through with weight over lead leg (9-13, 14).

9-4   9-5   9-6

8-16   9-1   8-17   9-2   9-3

9-7   9-8   9-9

9-10   9-11   9-12

10. Billy Pierce SET POSITION

Foot is on left side of rubber, palms facing belt. He raises his hands and lead leg simultaneously (10-2), which helps keep his weight back, reduces the chances of rushing. Correct lead arm action (10-4). Path of arm is down, back, and up correctly (10-3—6), but notice Billy does not emphasize "forward wrist" (10-4). High elbow (10-7). Excellent follow-through (10-9).

10-4   10-5   10-6

9-13   10-1

9-14   10-2   10-3

10-7   10-8   10-9

11. Bob Shaw SET POSITION

I had a slightly open stance (11-1) as did Wynn; we both had three-quarter-arm deliveries. Koufax and Pierce dropped their back shoulders more than I did because they threw overhand and I threw three-quarter-arm and rolled into the pitch, keeping my shoulders more level with the ground (11-5). They picked their lead legs up higher, which can be done by an overhand pitcher. Hands rise slightly as lead leg lifts up (11-3). "Forward wrist" (11-5). Path of arm is down, back, and up (11-5—7). Notice no pitchers illustrated threw with arm hooked behind the body. Correct lead arm action (11-6, 7). Ball of foot lands with throwing arm back and shoulder closed (11-7, 8). High elbow (11-10). Lead leg is bent, making it easy to bend at the waist and complete follow-through (11-13, 14).

11-4 **11-5** **11-6**

11-10 **11-11** **11-12**

11-1

11-2

11-3

11-7

11-8

11-9

11-13

11-14

IV / Coming to Grips with the Baseball

P-60AI

P-60AII

Even in professional ranks I have heard very little discussion of the correct way to grip a baseball. Many pitchers grip the ball wrong. Of course, the shape and size of each pitcher's hand are different. Nevertheless, the following basic fundamentals of grip are significant. The ball should be held as far out on the fingertips as comfortably possible, but don't have your fingers stiff or straight. Also, do not have your index and middle fingers too far apart. The thumb is tucked underneath the ball, between the index and middle fingers. The ball rests on the upper edge of the thumb. If the thumb is bent rather than kept straight, the wrist snap is reduced and the pressure point, instead of being toward the fingertips, as it should be, is farther back. Gripping the ball incorrectly with the thumb also causes a drag on the ball (P-60A I, II—correct; P-60B I, II—incorrect).

The middle finger is the most important of the two fingers that grip the ball, mainly because it is longer than the index finger and is the last finger in contact with the ball. It is generally the middle finger that controls the curve, slider, sinker, and fast ball. There is an exception in the case of the slider, which will be discussed later.

80

1. Tightness of Grip

During the preliminary motion the ball should be held loosely. If you hold the ball tight, the muscles of the forearm that are contracting will become tired in a very short time. Over-all tension can radiate throughout the entire body as a result of gripping the ball too tight.

The tighter you grip the ball, the more restricted your wrist snap becomes. However, the tighter you grip the ball, the faster the ball will spin. There is an analogy between hitting and pitching here. The experienced hitter holds the bat loosely and then when he starts his swing he automatically, unconsciously firms up his grip. In pitching, start by holding the ball loosely. I believe you will automatically tighten your grip as you go into the release area.

Some pitching coaches believe that a pitcher who is throwing high should grip the ball tighter so that he holds onto the ball longer and makes the ball go low. Conversely, they believe, a pitcher who is pitching low should loosen up on the ball. Personally, I think this is a stop-gap way of helping someone and doesn't get to the heart of his particular problem.

Remember, control depends on breaking the hands properly, proper lead leg action, keeping the elbow high to get on a downward plane, not rushing, and so on and so on.

The firmness of the grip should be constant, to give you the best feel of the ball.

2. Two Basic Grips

The two basic ways to grip are across the seams (P-61A), with the seams (P-61B).

As a general rule a person who throws extremely

P-60BI

P-60BII

81

hard overhand has more advantages throwing across the seams. The ball will be easier to control, and it will look smaller coming toward home plate. When you spin the ball across the seams, the seams blend together, making the ball look smaller. If you can apply enough spin and velocity when gripping the ball across the seams, you can overcome the downward force of gravity and make the ball rise.

Whereas throwing across the seams produces vertical or upward movement, throwing with the seams usually produces more lateral movement. All sinker-ball pitchers throw with the seams and usually throw from a three-quarter position. When you throw with the seams, there is generally more movement. You are utilizing gravity, and sometimes, the easier you throw, the more the ball moves. And the ball is moving down, away from the eyes and away from the plane of the bat, so you will get more ground balls than with an overhand delivery.

Generally speaking, the overhand cross-seam pitcher will be effective down as well as up, but the three-quarter-arm pitcher, with the seams, will find himself not so effective high because the ball has a tendency to go straight.

Just as the size and shape of the hands vary, so do grips. Experiment to find out which feels and works best for you. I believe youngsters should start across the seams. As they get older they can experiment and, if they lack an exceptional fast ball, go with the seams. These two grips are by far the most common. Whichever feels better and you get the best movement with is the one for you.

There are two additional grips you might want to try (P-62A, B). It is best to have fingers and thumb in contact with a seam. In these two grips your thumb probably will not touch a seam.

P-61A

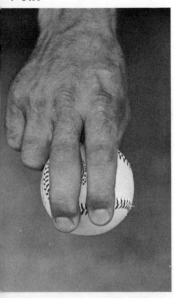

P-61B

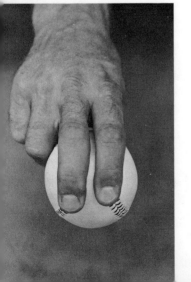

82

3. What Makes a Ball Move

Many years ago a scientist named Daniel Bernoulli discovered that the pressure of a fluid (liquid or gas) decreases at points where speed increases. In other words, Bernoulli found that within the same gas high-speed flow is associated with low pressure. As a base-ball moves through the air—which is a gas—it will move in the direction of the least pressure. This is why spin is so important: *The faster the spin, the better the movement* (I-11). And the direction of the spin determines the direction of the break.

At a high altitude the air is less dense, and the ball will not move so well—for example, in Denver, Colorado.

A breaking ball will move better in damp air than in dry air.

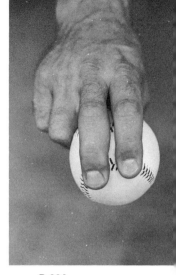

P-62A

P-62B

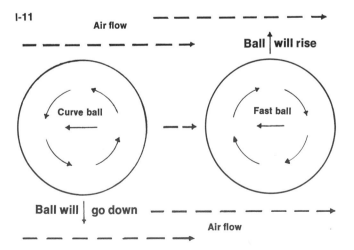

I-11

Air flow

Ball will rise

Curve ball

Fast ball

Ball will go down

Air flow

V / The Various Pitches

We have said that there are two basic grips, across the seams and with the seams. It is best to grip all your pitches the same. Many pitchers hold a fast ball one way and a curve ball another, but this system involves switching grips and may make it easier for the opposition to detect your different pitches. If you find you have much better stuff when you use different grips on different pitches, I suggest you start with your pitching hand in the glove during your preliminary motion.

1. Fast Ball

The cross-seam fast ball is thrown overhand, and you try to ride the ball. Your hand is directly behind the ball. The ball leaves the fingertip of the middle finger (P-63).

The sinker is considered a fast ball. How do you make the ball sink? We previously mentioned that the ball moves if the pitching arm moves from one extreme to the other. The ball will move in the opposite direction. This is why a sinker-ball pitcher usually uses a three-quarter-arm delivery. The ball leaves the

84

middle finger on the outside of the finger. The wrist is cocked slightly to the left, and the fingers are tipped away from your body, as illustrated (P-64).

Here is a suggestion by Freddie Martin, pitching coach with the Chicago Cubs organization, to help your sinker: When you throw with the seams, do not put your middle finger directly on top of the seam but place it to the left of the seam. When you look at the ball in your hand you should be able to see the seam to the right of your middle finger. Put your thumb on the seam as illustrated in the picture (P-65). Freddie Martin has helped numerous pitchers with their sinkers by this particular grip. It so happens that this is the grip that I used, and I was known as a sinker-ball pitcher.

You must avoid rotating the wrist to the right, or clockwise, which would cause the fast ball to move like a slider. If all pitches break in the same direction, it is most difficult to work in and out, trying to set up the hitter. It is advisable to have the fast ball go in to a hitter, and the curve and slider go away from a hitter (assuming that a right-handed pitcher is facing a right-handed hitter).

Don't attempt to throw two different types of fast balls—for example, a rising fast ball (across the seams) and a sinking fast ball (with the seams). In theory the plan sounds great, but in practical application it usually does more harm than good. You have to use different deliveries to accomplish this, and if you throw from two positions, your over-all control will be less than if you stayed with one delivery. Pitching is control. Establish a groove. Throw your fast ball one way and stay in one spot in your delivery. Yes, Juan Marichal is the exception. He can throw from any position and has great control. There are very few Marichals, however.

I repeat, throw from one spot.

85

P-64

P-65

P-66A

P-66B

PITCHING

2. Curve Ball

Years ago, terms like "drop," "downer," "out-shoot" were used to describe the curve ball. A curve ball by an overhand pitcher will break mostly down. A curve ball by a three-quarter-arm pitcher will break down and over. The curve is thrown with the elbow up. This is a must! It gives you the full radius of the circle, allows you to get on a downward plane, and increases hand speed. The size of the break is not as important as the angle of the break and the sharpness of the break. A ball breaking down, away from the plane of the bat, is most important.

There are a number of typical grips: across the seams and with the seams, as previously shown; and the horseshoe grip and the Maglie grip (P-66A, B).

How to throw the curve ball properly: Let's start with the grip. Whether you grip with or across the seams is not important. Obtaining spin is the most important thing for a good curve. Start by holding the ball loosely in your hand with fingers close together, the pressure is applied by the middle finger and the thumb (P-67). Do not grip the ball tightly with your thumb or you will restrict your wrist snap. The curve ball leaves the middle finger at the extreme end, or last section. To help break the ball straight down, rather than flat, try to release the ball as close to the middle knuckle of the middle finger as possible (P-68). All you are actually doing is hooking the ball with your fingers a little more to create a downward spin.

You think fast ball as you break your hands, and as you come up to the release area you go to the curve ball. There are two points of view as to where you start to position your hand for the curve. Most people say that the palm should face you and the hand should be cocked in slightly as you come into the

86

P-67

P-68

P-69A

P-69B

P-69C

P-69D

release area. You follow through, snapping your wrist down, with the ball rolling over your middle finger.

Johnny Sain, who is recognized as an outstanding pitching coach and authority on the breaking pitch, has a slightly different approach to the curve. He says, "You think fast ball all the way till you get slightly in front of your head." The palm is facing the hitter. Then you go to the curve ball by snapping your hand forward and down so that the back of the hand is facing the batter. This gives you maximum wrist action. The ball will leave the hand over the outer joint of the middle finger, where the nail is (P-69A, B, C, D).

P-70A

P-70B

P-70C

P-70D

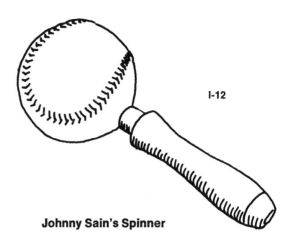

I-12

Johnny Sain's Spinner

Johnny Sain also feels that when you wrap the curve ball too soon, you lose hand speed; the more you cock your hand, the more you lock the wrist, which retards wrist snap. And he also feels you increase the margin of error by cocking the wrist too soon, making it difficult to be consistent. His method will give you not necessarily a bigger curve, but one that is quicker and sharper.

Other points to emphasize are these:

All good curve-ball pitchers throw with the elbow up. This gives you hand speed, allows you to pull down to impart better spin, and also allows you to start the ball on a downward plane, so it will break down sharply away from the plane of the bat. (The phrase "Karate chop" best describes the hand acceleration required for a good curve ball.) (P-70A, B, C, D.)

To help increase the spin when you pull down with your fingers, flip up with your thumb. To aid in learning the proper spin for the curve and other pitches, Johnny Sain has developed a Spinner (I-12). (If you want to purchase a Spinner, write: John Sain, Box 487, Walnut Ridge, Arkansas 72476.)

PITCHING

Correct wrist action will prevent injury to the elbow. Incorrect wrist action—rotating forearm and wrist to the right—puts undue strain on the elbow, increases the chance of injury, and causes a flat curve (I-13).

The hand should try to stay ahead of the elbow. Don't intentionally try to lead with the elbow (P-71 —incorrect). In the action photos you will see that the elbow leads the arm until you get to the release area; then the hand catches up with the elbow quickly and passes it. This is how and where hand speed is developed, provided the elbow is up.

Pitchers who wrap the curve ball too soon generally bring the hand too close to the head instead of having the arm perpendicular to the ground. It is difficult to get consistency with your curve when you wrap it next to your ear, and the pitch will generally be a slow curve that starts uphill. This type of delivery makes you lift with your shoulder, creating a greater margin of error. Your control will be off and you will find it difficult to maintain a groove (P-72).

Reach out and follow through so that your throwing hand finishes down past your left thigh to achieve a better curve and maintain the groove (P-73).

The question is often asked: At what age should a youngster start throwing a curve ball? In my ex-

P-71

P-72

P-73

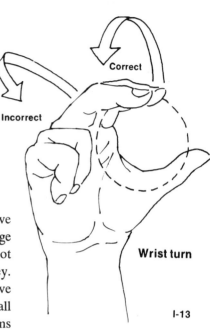

Correct

Incorrect

Wrist turn

I-13

perience, most of the good curve-ball pitchers have started young. You can injure your arm at any age if you do not throw the curve correctly. Age is not the factor. Proper planning and program are the key. The coach should explain the mechanics of the curve ball, start slowly, and have the pitcher spin the ball at half-speed. He should make sure the pitcher warms up properly before attempting to throw hard. The youngster should have the coordination and strength to attempt these pitches, and proper supervision of the program to prevent abuse of his arm.

But remember, a boy can hurt his arm throwing fast balls just as easily as he can throwing curves.

Tip: When first learning to throw curve balls, begin throwing easily from a short distance. Get the spin down first; spin is everything. As you perfect the spin, move farther and farther away, until you have arrived at the regulation distance, and watch the spin of the ball. *Start slow and easy*. Practice finger action for the curve. Snap the thumb and middle finger. You can also practice the curve with the ball in your hand by flipping the ball in the air as you snap your finger, producing a rapid spin.

91

P-74A   P-74B

P-74C

3. Slider or Fast Curve Ball

The expression "nickel curve" often crops up. The big-league pitcher who is making a big salary doesn't use the term "nickel curve"; he uses the term "slider." More correctly, it should be called "fast curve" or "hard curve."

Actually a slider is a curve ball, but it looks like a fast ball with a quick break at the end. The use of the slider in modern days is probably one of the reasons for the decline of the .300 hitter.

A word of caution should be given regarding the slider. In professional baseball the manager generally asks, when a home run is hit, "What was the pitch?" Many times the reply is, "Slider." With that, the manager will make a funny, distorted face and cringe. If you had said, "Fast ball," or, "Curve," his reaction would have been only half as bad.

Although a slider is a curve in terminology, the differences between the two are that the slider is much faster than the curve, the break is sharper, and it breaks much later. Remember to break the slider down, not over. Because of the tremendous speed, the break is not as big as the break of the curve. As far as I have observed, fewer mistakes are made with the slider than with the curve. Most of the big winners use the slider because it is easier to control and the ideal pitch to use when you are behind the hitter on the count.

One of the best teachers of the slider is Whitlow Wyatt. His method produced many pitchers with outstanding sliders. The slider is thrown with the wrist turned slightly to the right. (Fast ball, hand behind the ball; slider, slight turn to the right; curve ball, quarter-turn, palm facing you—P-74A, B, C.) As in the curve ball, the pressure is between the thumb and middle finger. The only difference is that there is less rotation to the right because you want forward

92

speed. If you turn your hand fully to the right you will come closer to the curve-ball position, causing too big a break and losing forward speed.

Hold the ball just the way you hold your fast ball. (The best slider is held across the seams because the spin is harder to detect. If you throw your fast ball with the seams, you will probably throw the slider the same way.) Then you are instructed to raise the index finger on the ball (P-75). The fingers are on top of the ball, not at the side. Keep the elbow up, keep the weight back, bring the arm across the body, try to keep the hand ahead of the elbow. When you raise the index finger, you automatically hold the ball off-center and the pressure is automatically and correctly applied to the inside of the middle finger. After you have worked with the slider awhile and gotten the feel, you will want to put the index finger back on the ball, but remember, very little pressure should be applied by the index finger. Use wrist action. It is incorrect to throw the slider with a stiff wrist.

Many methods are used in teaching the slider. Hold the ball off-center. I do not like this method of teaching the slider because it gives an altogether different feel to the ball. It is harder to control.

Johnny Sain's method of teaching the slider is as follows. He starts the pitcher off by asking him to throw the fast ball and give him back spin. The pitcher actually pulls down with both fingers, with wrist action imparting back spin. Then Sain asks the pitcher to turn his hand *slightly* to the right (clockwise) and give him back spin. The result is a hard slider. There is no strain on the elbow, velocity is maintained, and because the pitch is so similar to the fast ball, it permits control and maintains the groove. Keep in mind that in this method you pull down with both fingers.

Personally, I had better results when I consciously

P-75

held the ball in the fingertips. It must be emphasized that the path of the arm should go *across the body* for the slider or fast curve. This is what pulls the ball over and down, giving the ball the proper spin.

Another method is to throw as if the ball were a football. I do not like this method because the break is too big; the ball breaks parallel to the bat. Forward speed is insufficient because your fingers are on the side of the ball, not on top, and wrist snap in this position puts an extra amount of strain on the elbow. The term "nickel curve" is appropriate for this type of pitch, and injury to the elbow often occurs (P-76A—incorrect; P-76B—correct).

The fingers should always be on top of the ball. The best illustration is in I-14. Hold the glove hand above your head, palm down; put the backs of your index and middle fingers against the palm of your hand. The illustration shows the positions: A—fast ball; B—slider; C—slurve, a pitch between a slider and a curve, with a bigger break than the slider; D—curve.

I have previously said that you should always break the ball down, out of the plane of the bat. There is one exception, and that pertains to the slider when a right-hander faces a left-handed hitter. When you break a slider down on the low inside part of the plate, you allow the hitter to put the sweet part of the bat on the ball, resulting in a hit down the right-field line. When you don't have to throw a strike, break the ball flat and inside, belt-high. Percentages are that the batter will hit the ball foul if he makes contact. This is a good way to jam the hitter.

The importance of the slider is recognized by astute baseball men: it is easy to learn and it can be thrown for a strike more consistently than the curve ball. It is especially important in a game situation when the count is 3–1, 3–2, or 2–0. The ability to

P-76A

P-76B

94

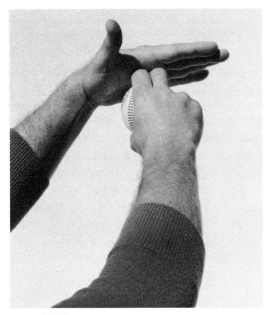

I-14A

I-14B

I-14C

I-14D

P-77

P-78A

P-78B

get a breaking pitch over consistently when you are behind in the count will make you a winning pitcher.

4. Slow Curve

The slow curve is a valuable pitch and is thrown exactly like the curve ball except easier. You might want to grip the ball not quite as hard as you do with the regular curve ball. You may want to try putting it farther back in your hand. As you know, hitting is timing, and the slow curve is used to throw the hitter's timing off. Some coaches teach dragging the rear leg on any type of change. You may want to try this on the slow curve.

5. Change-Up

The motion for the change-up should look exactly like that for the fast ball. The change-up is one pitch that will require much experimentation. There are many ways to try to throw it.

One is to hold the ball loosely; using less effort, throw just the same as the fast ball, with the same grip, letting the ball come off both fingers or the outside part of the middle finger. Be sure to hold on to the ball longer; emphasize bringing your arm across your body. This method is usually used by a three-quarter-arm pitcher (P-77).

In another method the ball is held slightly back in your hand. Raise the fingertips off the ball; pressure is applied between thumb and middle joints of the index and middle fingers. As you learn this change, the fingers don't have to be held straight up. The ball comes off the raised fingers spinning just like the fast ball. The expression "pulling the shade" best explains the path of the right hand, but be sure to let the ball go way out in front and keep the hand back

96

—no wrist action (P-78A, B). The Dodgers have taught this method for years. Carl Erskine and Johnny Podres both had great changes. This method is used by overhand pitchers.

For a third way, hold the ball far back in the hand. This causes drag, so it is impossible to throw the ball hard. This is called the palm ball. I believe this method is the most difficult to master (P-79).

A three-finger delivery will help reduce wrist snap and was the easiest for me to master (P-80).

A good change-up requires a great deal of practice. The thing to guard against is slowing up the arm action going into the release area. This will give the pitch away. Drag the right foot or leave it back; this may help, although it hasn't worked for me. A change-up is a good pitch against certain hitters. Fast arm action is the key to throwing it.

Two suggestions: Guard against speeding up your preliminary motion. And it is dangerous to throw a change-up to a power hitter whose power is to right center and left center because it allows him with little or no adjustment to pull the ball out of the park down the line.

6. Slip Pitch

The slip pitch is a form of change-up but is slightly different because the spin is not the same as on the fast ball, but it accomplishes the same thing as the straight change. The ball is held slightly back in the hand, pressure at the first knuckle of the thumb, and slightly back in the index and middle fingers, not in the fingertips. The hand is rotated to the right in a position as if you were throwing a football (P-81). No wrist action; keep your hand back. It is almost impossible to throw the ball hard. In a brief conversation I had with Paul Richards during spring training,

P-79   P-80

P-81

97

P-82A

P-82B

P-82C

he made the following comment: "A sound delivery is most important. If a pitcher is unable to master a straight change, which is often the case, then the slip pitch has proved a good way to learn the change." The slip pitch has made winners out of a number of pitchers under Richards.

Here are four suggestions that may help. Try getting your pitching hand up more quickly. Try to bring the pitching hand through before the left foot lands. Bring the pitching hand way over to the left. Throw just as hard as you can, and don't use any wrist action. (Don't be discouraged when you first start.)

When I ask about the slip pitch, some pitchers remark that they experience a strain on the elbow. Each individual pitcher must determine whether this is the right pitch for him.

7. Screwball

The screwball is thrown with spin opposite to that of a curve, so that the ball from a right-hander will break down and away from a left-handed hitter. It is an excellent change-of-speed pitch, most effective if used by a right-handed pitcher against a left-handed hitter or by a left-handed pitcher against a right-handed hitter.

Don't consciously lift your shoulder to throw the screwball. The elbow is used as a fulcrum. The ball comes off the outside of the middle finger. Get the fingers up on top so that the ball will break down and away (P-82A, B, C).

8. Knuckle Ball

The knuckle ball actually should be called the fingertip ball because it is gripped with the fingertips. Most knuckle-ball pitchers drop the elbow and push the ball out with the wrist held back.

98

Hoyt Wilhelm is probably the greatest knuckle-ball pitcher of all time. He delivers the ball with his elbow up and says he does flip the ball out with his fingers and wrist. Try not to have your fingers touch a seam. The best result is when the ball makes a quarter-turn toward home plate as it travels. The best way to practice the knuckle ball is to stand close to someone and try to have no spin on the ball as you throw to him (P-83A, B).

porating the knuckle ball in his repertoire. However, if you have limited ability or need an extra pitch and can throw a knuckle ball, by all means let the good times roll.

P-83B

9. Fork Ball

The fork ball is practically an impossibility for some people to throw because their first and middle fingers will not separate far enough. The purpose of the fork ball is to reduce the spin and it generally spins in reverse, causing it to go down (P-84).

The following pitches are mentioned for general information only. I do *not* recommend their use.

Spitball: The spitball has received much notoriety in recent years. Actually, very few pitchers have used it since it was banned many years ago. In many instances it has hurt a pitcher rather than helped him, because he didn't know how to throw it properly.

P-84

The late Frank Shellenback, who was one of the last pitchers to be allowed to throw the spitball legally, explained to me how it was done. Slippery elm was used to make the consistency of the saliva slick. Thayer's Slippery Elm Lozenges are far superior to just slippery-elm bark. A spot on the ball is prepared. On every ball there will be a trademark or name. The pitcher spits into the left hand and

99

then rubs the slippery-elm saliva into the leather to prepare the ball. Everyone thinks he is rubbing up the entire ball. Actually he rubs only one spot. He then goes to his mouth to get some saliva on his fingertips, grips the ball where there are no seams, and puckers the ball, forcing the ball into the fingertips. The pitcher must be sure to pop the wrist forward. He cannot be lazy with his wrist.

From what I hear from some of the pitchers who have thrown the spitball, it feels like a watermelon seed popping out between your fingers. Because your fingers are wet and thumb is dry, the ball comes out spinning in reverse. The ball is thrown hard and will go down if thrown overhand, and down and away if thrown with a three-quarter-arm delivery. The old-time spitball pitchers used to say, "Prepare, pucker, and pop."

Since the rule was passed not allowing you to go to your mouth while on the rubber, almost all spitball pitchers have switched to water-soluble KY petroleum jelly, which is placed on some part of the uniform, belt, hair, et cetera.

Mudball: If you want to experiment and see a ball explode, wet a portion of the ball and grind the ball into the dirt. If you throw the ball with the spot up, the ball will move down; if the spot is on the side the ball will move laterally. It will always move in the direction opposite to the dirt, or a nick, scrape, or cut. A scuffed or cut ball will really move if the pitcher knows how to utilize it properly.

Pine tar is used by some pitchers to get a better grip. This may help with the curve ball.

Some pitchers still attempt to mark and nick a ball by rubbing it against the belt buckle, which is shaped or sharpened for this purpose. I doubt if emery paper is being used in this day and age to scuff up the ball.

VI / Teaching Methods

There is one basic assumption to remember about teaching: it should be slow, one idea at a time. A suggestion is easier to put across than a "must" or a hard-and-fast rule. There are many different types of individuals. Teaching should be a continued, organized, progressive program. Repetition and constant supervision are essential. A good teacher must be patient, understanding, and knowledgeable.

The reason there are very few good coaches is that few know the intricate mechanics of pitching and realize the importance of constant repetition and constant supervision. Just mentioning a point a few times will not get the desired results. Constant daily supervision is necessary.

It must be remembered that a new art, movement, or skill seems unnatural at first because you have not educated the muscles and nerves. The brain has not yet accepted it. The kinesthetic sense must be developed.

The statement so often heard, "It doesn't feel comfortable," is truthful but should be avoided in the vocabulary of the aspiring pitcher who is seeking human perfection. The concern of always feeling comfortable or natural will have to be discarded. Only after you have learned the correct method or movement and have used it many times, will it feel natural and comfortable. Your old way will then feel uncomfortable.

Some individuals learn quickly and some don't. The person who learns slowly should be encouraged to spend more time to learn a specific fundamental. Break the fundamental skill down to the smallest component part. If possible, put the component part into a game or exercise. Then, as each part is mastered, it can be fitted with the others.

A good teacher will encourage the individual and let him know when signs of improvement are apparent. The average person generally looks for a way out when things go badly and will put the blame on someone else. We all do this at times, but it is wrong. Instead of complaining and griping, develop an attitude of "What can I do to make myself a better pitcher?" Rather than blaming a hard-nosed teacher, face up to your own liabilities and shortcomings.

The teacher must evaluate the pupil pitcher under the following categories: 1) ability; 2) aptitude; 3) intelligence; 4) desire and drive; 5) personality; 6) ability to concentrate; 7) determination; 8) physical make-up; 9) strength; 10) intestinal fortitude. If the individual hasn't got the ability, "you can't get blood out of a stone."

Most people want to learn and improve their skills. The reason so many fail is that in the beginning of the learning process there is always a period where you seemingly do not improve. The instant cure is rare. As in golf, most youngsters go under the wing of a professional and put in days, weeks, months, and usually years under constant supervision to achieve mechanical perfection.

When the mechanics have been mastered, there is the mental aspect to consider.

Al Campanis, vice-president of the Los Angeles Dodgers, has compiled information on methods of teaching which is significant enough to repeat here. Following are some typical learning problems he points out.

> When an instructor feels that he is not "getting through" to a player, the difficulty may come from a number of causes other than lack of effort, native ability, or interest.

Here are three common kinds of difficulty:

1. *Misunderstanding:* The learner sees in his mind's eye something different from what the instructor has in mind.

Certain words or phrases may mean different things to the learner than they do to the instructor. Or they mean very little at all, because the learner lacks certain necesary *experiences*. Words must be backed up by something more specific, which provides the necessary experiences and a common basis of understanding.

Teaching aids that provide such specific experiences are:

    a) The explanation, demonstration, and partici-pation method
    b) Lectures
    c) Diagrams
    d) Slow-motion pictures
    e) Equipment
    f) Visual Aids

2. *Forgetting:* The learner understands but he cannot remember. He forgets how he released the curve ball. Bad habits of the past make him lapse back to dropping his arm, and consequently he throws a flat curve. "The laws of learning" indicate that learning is not a continuous upward movement or improvement. There are temporary setbacks or dropbacks. At this point, the instructor must exercise patience and good judgment. An explanation to the player that it is not uncommon to go through a temporary learning drop-back is important. Encouragement or "a pat on the back" is also indicated. After all, animal trainers (who are considered expert teachers) give their animals some

sugar after performing each feat or trick. We should "sugar up" our players more. Praise is an effective and important tool in teaching.

3. *Mental block or resistance:* The learner feels under pressure, because he is unable to follow and feels inferior, or "on the spot"—and so he blocks or resists.

The learner who has missed *even an unimportant point* along the way may be lost without knowing why. If he is learning in a group, the pressure to keep up and the humiliation of looking bad before others may make him so anxious that he becomes confused—so he defends his self-esteem with the attitude that "This is a lot of bull, what good is it!" etc. The remedy: Skilled, private, individual instruction and review, without pressure but with encouragement for every step successfully completed. But individual instruction may be impractical because it takes too much time, or too much manpower is needed (Dodgertown). In that case, textbook study is one form of individual instruction that removes pressure by letting the learner proceed at his own rate, without humiliation or embarrassment.

Pressure: We have all heard the expression, he "choked." This term is used loosely and it is exaggerated. I don't believe any player "chokes." He may be trying too hard, he may be lacking in fundamental play, or he may have *not as yet learned* how to accept the pressure or tension of a tight situation or game. Managers and coaches must exercise care in not showing disapproval because of a young player's failure in a given situation. This will only tend to tighten him up in the future. Let's not compound the ordinary pressure. Improvement in many players can be traced to their learning how to accept pressure. Consequently, we must assume that handling pressure is learnable. The necessary ingredients are:

1. Positive thinking. 2. Constant encouragement.

Tip: In learning something new, the pitcher should exaggerate the movement; otherwise he will drift back to his old way quickly.

VII / Teaching Aids

A coach should use teaching aids wherever possible. They will help break up the monotony and speed up the learning process.

1. Figure Eight

The figure eight has already been mentioned. It will help teach timing and rhythm with regard to the arms and trunk rotation. Do it at home in your spare time. Think "up-down" so that by repetition it becomes automatic. Remember, you want to re-educate your muscles. Constant repetition of the correct movements will do the job.

2. Broom Handle

Another teaching aid is a broom handle. It should be held far enough in front so that the hand doesn't hit it (P-85). It will force the pitcher to get the arm up and throw down and over it. He will be pitching on a downward plane and will have to keep his weight back. The motion is very close to that of spiking a volley ball over a net. Remember that the pitching arm goes up-down. The broom handle should be high enough to force the arm to be ex-

P-85

105

tended upward. The pitcher will be forced to break his hands quickly and get the arm down, back, and up. He will not collapse. It will be awkward to kick the leg back. In fact, this exercise will force the pitcher to execute most of the basic fundamentals automatically.

3. Mirror

Pitching in front of a mirror is most beneficial in that you can see for yourself if you are performing properly. Only by repeating the correct movements over and over again will you get the feeling of pitching in a mechanically correct way, and in time these movements will become automatic. This is important because when pitching in competition you must concentrate on the target. You cannot think of two things at the same time. I repeat, *go through the correct movements in front of the mirror until they become second nature to you.*

P-86

4. Canvas Backstop

The best way to practice is throwing to a catcher, who moves the glove in and out, up and down, giving a specific target. If a catcher isn't available, a canvas may be used, with the spots painted on it (P-86). *Always throw at a specific target.* Never start your preliminary motion until your eyes have seen the specific spot and you have drawn an imaginary picture in your mind of the path of the ball to that specific target.

5. Motion Pictures

The use of a slow-motion camera can also be a tremendous help. Any time you can see yourself, you

106

generally get a better idea of what you have to correct and what should be done. Remember the proverb, "One picture is worth a thousand words."

Eight-mm. film is less expensive and just as good as 16-mm.

6. Indian Drill

To learn "high elbow" and "forward wrist," the pitcher should sit on the ground with legs crossed and throw to another person sitting in like position. Start ten or fifteen feet apart and work back (P-87). You may accomplish the same thing by throwing on your knees.

P-87

7. Pick Up Dirt

When learning follow-through, remember "toe to toe." The instruction "Pick up grass or dirt after you throw the ball" will force the student pitcher to bend the front leg and bend at the waist and complete the follow-through.

8. Hat Trick

When a pitcher is continually high, place your cap halfway between the mound and home plate. Ask the pitcher to hit the cap and bounce the ball to the catcher. You are forcing the pitcher to do what is necessary to keep the ball low.

9. Diagrams on Wall

Putting adhesive tape on the wall will teach the proper path of the arm and help prevent movement of the head (I-15).

10. Stopwatch

Goldie Holt, coach in the Dodger organization, showed me how beneficial timing a pitcher with a stopwatch from a set position can be. We clocked the pitcher from the time he started his delivery till the ball crossed the plate. A pitcher should unload the ball in less than one second. This system makes a contest or game out of the exercise for the pitchers. It is amazing the improved results you can get.

Many players practice what they do best; good players practice what they do poorly.
    Many pitchers throw against a wall. This is not a good way to learn. You often throw on an upward plane rather than a downward plane in order to get the ball to bounce back. Always work off a mound with a catcher whenever possible.
    Also, when throwing balls in from the outfield be sure to throw correctly. Bad habits are formed if you get lazy or fool around when throwing from the outfield or playing catch on the sidelines.

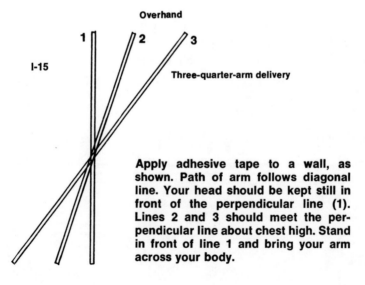

Overhand

1   2   3

I-15

Three-quarter-arm delivery

Apply adhesive tape to a wall, as shown. Path of arm follows diagonal line. Your head should be kept still in front of the perpendicular line (1). Lines 2 and 3 should meet the perpendicular line about chest high. Stand in front of line 1 and bring your arm across your body.

VIII / Mental Aspects of Pitching

1. Concentration

To be outstanding in anything, you must learn to concentrate. This means directing your entire mental capacity on a specific objective. Your objective as a pitcher is to throw the ball where you want it to go. Steps in the right direction are keeping your head up, looking at the target from start to finish in your delivery, focusing on the minute spot over the plate where you want the ball to go (specifically, the center of the pocket of the catcher's glove). You must not allow yourself the luxury of letting your mind think of anything else but where you are going to throw the ball. The mind, the muscles, the concentration, and the proper mechanics with the downward plane will enable you to do what you want with the baseball.

You can concentrate on only one thing at a time properly. The area of focus of the eyes is limited to a very small spot. Therefore your mind and eyes cannot wander from their determination to throw the ball to a definite spot.

On each pitch, you have four things to do, in this order:

(a) Concentrate on where you want to throw the pitch.

(b) Throw the ball hard, using your maximum stuff.

(c) Protect yourself.

(d) Field your position.

Some managers fine a pitcher for letting a ball go through the mound when the manager thinks it should have been caught or fielded by the pitcher. This system makes the pitcher concentrate on fielding his position. But if he is concentrating on fielding, he is not concentrating on where he will throw the ball. More important, he may not put maximum effort into the pitch. The end result may be that he doesn't have to field his position as he watches the ball go out of the park.

2. Mind Power

Concentration is not easy and requires practice. Learning to concentrate also means developing your memory. To remember incidents, events, situations, routines, routine progression, in their order and time of happening—this is mind power. This does not mean that you have to have a photographic memory. This mind power can be developed by constantly challenging your mind to perform these mental gymnastics. For example, a chess-player should be able to remember all his moves and the moves of his opponent and project his thinking to future moves. You also can develop mind power by playing cards—for example, bridge, hearts, and gin rummy. Mind power can be increased through golf, with the ability to remember the course, position of shots, distances, clubs used, and grain of different greens. Most human beings do not realize and capitalize on the full capacity of their brains.

To help his memory, a pitcher should keep notes on each opponent in his league. These notations should consist of pertinent data with regard to hitting weaknesses and individual idiosyncrasies. For example, is he a fast-ball hitter or a better curve-ball hitter? Does he handle the ball up or down, in or out, better? Does he hit better with men on base or not? Is he overanxious to swing with men on base? Is he a guess hitter? Is he a first-ball hitter? All these notations will help the pitcher, because it is most difficult to remember all these characteristics. Hitters change from year to year and game to game. Mind power is limited; therefore a black book is a must and should be kept up to date. When you first come into a league in organized baseball, there are twenty-five players on each team and twelve teams in a league. There will be approximately three hundred hitters to remember. I repeat, in the beginning a book is a must. As the years go by, it may not be needed if you are blessed with an outstanding memory.

3. Relaxation

Relax physically but never mentally. If you are tense, control and timing are impossible. Learning to relax is a must, but for some of us it will take a long time to master tension. The desire to do good and to impress can be a negative force, hurt you rather than help you. Here are a couple of suggestions that may help you relax. Take a deep breath before you start your motion, let the air out and let yourself go limp. Tense all your muscles and then let them go.

4. Mental Attitude

Having the proper mental attitude is probably the most important part of successful pitching.

If you are confident you can do the job without fear of failure, you usually don't tense up. Confidence is developed only by having successful outings. You never develop confidence by doing things wrong and having little or no success. If you want to be a successful pitcher, you must pitch mechanically right, be strong and flexible, pitch every chance you can to improve yourself, gain confidence, and learn to relax. Don't muscle up or grit your teeth. Coaches use the expression "loosey goosey" or "be a rag doll."

Proper mental attitude is the basis for success in any player. It consists of the will to win, eagerness to learn, and the intelligence to retain what you have learned from experience. If what you did yesterday still looks big to you, you haven't done much today.

It is a normal tendency to try extra hard when members of your family, your girl friend, scouts, or club officials are in attendance, when you are trying to impress, or when it is a very important game. Trying to throw too hard, you generally rush and create nothing but problems. Learn to relax and concentrate.

5. Positive Thinking

This was part of the title of a successful book by Norman Vincent Peale. He believes that without the proper mental attitude or approach you cannot succeed, because the mind controls the body. The pitcher must have the proper mental attitude toward the batter. The batter is your enemy, with certain strengths and certain weaknesses, which you should know. The greatest hitter who ever lived averaged only one hit every three times up. Let these statistics build up your confidence. The pitcher always has the advantage over the hitter, percentagewise.

Think these things positively:

I can learn the proper mechanics, and I will practice until I grasp them.

I can develop my body physically. I can endure pain, and I'm willing to sacrifice certain pleasures now, because in the end I will be rewarded in many ways—financially and personally.

I can develop myself mentally through study, and I have self-discipline to do what I know is necessary.

Say, "I can and will throw on a downward plane," rather than, "Gee, that feels funny and uncomfortable; I've done pretty well the other way." Never accept mediocrity. Think positive—be the best!

Remember, the mind controls the body. What's the sense of being strong physically and weak mentally? Be strong both ways.

6. Aggressiveness

I feel sorry for the individual who lacks aggressiveness. Many people are born this way and, although most are probably well liked, they never seem to get anywhere. I hate to say it, but experience as a coach has shown me that I am almost wasting my time with a man who lacks aggressiveness. You can always tone somebody down, but it is almost impossible to put the spark in him to make him aggressive.

The person who reads this book and nods his head and says, "Very interesting," will probably get nowhere in this cruel world. By now you should have moved the coffee table over or turned the television off and started to see if what I say actually works. You have to put the book down on the lawn and start throwing. The aggressive person does not wait for success to come to him; he goes out of his way to get it and will fight on even against so-called insurmountable odds.

7. Emotional Stability

Controlling your emotions is something you must constantly work on, on and off the playing field.

113

Some people stomp around, hit things, throw things, holler, show disgust, or sulk when things go wrong. All of these actions accomplish very little. For example, I saw a young aspiring pitcher with an abundance of ability break his hand by punching a wall after being removed from a game. He was out for the rest of the year and could have ruined his career. Anger robs the individual of the ability to concentrate.

A serious, expressionless face and calm, unhurried actions should be constant when things go badly and when things go well. It is very important for the young aspiring pitcher to remember this. It is not easy to achieve these things. They happen to be one phase of pitching that I had a hard time mastering. Certainly, after winning, a big smile is in order. But hat-throwing and so on are for the juvenile. Firm handshakes in the clubhouse with your teammates are more appropriate. When you lose, don't sulk or blame someone else. Find out what you did wrong, study the game, and profit by your mistakes.

Your attitude and your approach to the game are most important in their effect on the opposition or enemy. Walk to the mound with your head up and with a look of assurance. If you take forever to get to the mound, with lazy steps and head down, you radiate the feeling: "Maybe I don't belong out here." Don't be cocky, but give an air of confidence. Easy double-time to the mound is not out of order. Show everyone that you have a job to do and you are ready to do it.

With a confident attitude, you think: I can get him to hit my pitch. I will not give in to him; I will battle him right down to the 3–2 pitch. I am not afraid to throw a curve for my 3–2 pitch. I can match my fast ball low to his strength. I can outthink his guessing.

8. Superstitions and Mannerisms

The fewer mannerisms and superstitions you have, the better off you will be. They can become a crutch to lean on, and they show lack of confidence. *Remember, any movement that doesn't have a purpose is wasted or a hindrance.*

9. Butterflies in Your Stomach

If you get scared, feel nervous, or have a sick feeling, don't worry about it. There were a couple of hundred thousand other guys who felt the same way long before you came along. It is a natural feeling for a highly competitive individual. In fact, if you lose it you are probably going downhill.

IX / Pitcher-Hitter Relationship

1. Attitude

A mental attitude toward the hitter must be established. For example, in football your attitude about an outstanding player is that he is mean and tough. In a body-contact sport like football, you must hit the opponent hard. Why? Because he's going to hit you hard. And generally the one that hits the hardest wins. In boxing, the attitude that you are going to beat your opponent to death is an exaggeration, but the aim is to beat him to submission.

The fact is that the hitter is the pitcher's enemy. Of course, as in all sports, this attitude does not include any intention of deliberately injuring or maiming an opponent.

Much has been written about the beanball. No one likes having a baseball thrown at his head. Only a psychopathic individual would deliberately try to injure a hitter by throwing at him. However, it is almost impossible to hit the hitter in the head with a pitch unless he is guessing a specific pitch or a pitch in a certain place. Most of the time, if a hitter gets hit in the head, it is his fault. Hitters who crowd the plate or stick their heads over the plate generally get hit more often. This is their fault. Pitch inside to move the hitter away from the plate—brush him back! Let's face it, this is what makes the game interesting. Does the hitter have the courage to stand in? Good hitters do. The hitters with less intestinal fortitude aren't playing in the big leagues.

Pitching is pitching a ball up and down and in and out. Many pitchers fail because they are afraid they might hit and injure a hitter. My suggestion to you is to forget the hitter, let him take care of himself. Why do I feel this way? Because I know that, unless you have extraordinary ability, the one thing that may get you by is your aggressiveness, your meanness, and, yes, your hatred for the hitter.

Do not forget that many hitters try to line the ball back at the pitcher, hit it up the middle. When he hits at you, the hitter is more interested in getting a base hit than he is in your welfare. So be aggressive when you pitch, and don't worry about hitting the hitter. If you have a reputation of not moving the batter back, you will give the batter one less thing to think about, and also an opportunity to dig in.

However, there are some hitters—very few, I might add—who become better hitters after they have been thrown at (Ted Williams and Al Kaline, to mention two).

2. Never Give In to the Hitter

This instruction requires an explanation. As you develop your mechanics and become a full-fledged pitcher with a fast ball, curve, and change of speed, the attitude of never giving in to the hitter is of paramount importance, especially in the big leagues. Don't give him the pitch he expects. For example, most hitters are confident and think they're going to get the fast ball with a count of 2–0 or 3–1. I'm not saying don't throw the fast ball, but if you do, make it to your strength or try to hit a specific spot.

117

In other words, don't just throw it over the plate to get a strike; get a low strike.

There are many things to consider. Will the manager put the take on? Know who the hitter is; some hitters just won't walk or can't lay off a bad pitch. What are the abilities of the hitter? Who follows him in the batting order? Is there an open base? And, naturally, remember the score of the game and the number of outs. Much of this is discussed later, when I take up strategy. Until you develop the attitude that you are not going to give in to the hitter in certain situations and give him the pitch he's looking for and wants, you will not be a consistent winner.

Pitching around a hitter means not giving in to the hitter under any circumstances and keeping the ball out of the strike zone. Try to make the hitter go after a bad ball.

There are generally two or three situations in every game where a pitcher has to throw caution to the winds and gamble. You either do or you don't. A good example is: bases loaded, 3–1 on the hitter. You must throw a strike. So relax and let her go.

3. Spot versus Area Pitching

All the outstanding winners in the big leagues have the ability to put the ball where they want it to go, whether they have a great fast ball or not. The instruction "Throw the ball hard, aim at the middle of the plate, and you'll pick up the corners" may produce quick temporary results for the high-school pitcher who wants to do a satisfactory job right now, but if a pitcher is interested in becoming an outstanding pitcher, the sooner he tries to hit a spot on each pitch the sooner he will achieve his goal. The illustration (I-16) shows home plate with ten inches of the middle blacked out. This area is called "death

I-16

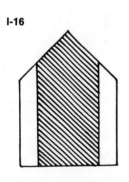

Death Valley

118

valley." Why? Simply because if you pitch over this area you are giving the hitter exactly what he wants. The more you pitch, the more you will find out that making pitches too good is your biggest problem.

For example, what does the young pitcher do with two strikes? The proper thing to do is throw the ball close enough to the plate to entice the hitter to swing. *Throwing strikes doesn't mean you have good control. The ability not to throw a strike is most important.*

Never throw a baseball unless you are pitching at a specific spot. Do not throw to a general area. When you pick a specific spot, the eyes focus on the spot, a picture is sent to the brain, and the brain sends a message to the hand to release the ball at a specific place. This is why you must learn correct mechanics, so that you have your body and arm under complete control. Concentration is essential for this process. When you have control, you are a pitcher, not a thrower, and a consistent winner.

4. Competitive Spirit

Do you have the competitive spirit? Most healthy people enjoy competition. It is natural to want to succeed and compete against your fellow man. Victory is sweet. Those who lack this drive should try to do something about it. Try to win at Ping-Pong, golf, badminton, cards, and darts. I hate to say it, but if you don't have competitive spirit, I doubt if you will make it to the top. Anyone can quit, but the greats take pride in their personal achievements.

Regarding the mental aspect of pitching, a book you may be interested in reading is *Psycho-Cybernetics* by Maxwell Maltz, M.D., F.I.C.S. It is available in paperback.

X / Strength and Flexibility

Great athletes possess strength and power combined with stamina and quick reflex action.

What is the difference between the Little Leaguer and the professional, aside from experience? The "little fellow" just doesn't have the size, strength, or stamina.

A youngster must realize that sitting in the movies, driving a car, or being entertained by television or radio is not going to make him a strong young man. He must counteract this sedentary life by vigorous, stimulating physical activity.

Years ago the average youngster engaged in manual labor. Many of the outstanding athletes were farmers or coal miners. Nowadays we must rely on calisthenics, flexibility-and-strength exercises, proper use of light weights, running, and so on, to achieve the necessary development of the muscles. *You must have strength to be great.* Supplement your everyday life with a specific program. Strength and flexibility exercises will fully develop your body.

When you use your muscles over and over again, you develop strength, and you also help the ligaments and tendons to adhere to the bone more securely. The more securely these are attached to the bone, the less will be your chance of injury. The more we use the muscles, the more endurance we have.

Strength is great, but without flexibility you are in serious trouble. Flexibility is suppleness, the ability to go through the range of motions without tension. For example, the track athlete does a tremendous number of flexibility exercises before he runs. If he cannot go through his range of motions without tension, there is no way he can be an outstanding runner. In pitching, if your legs are not flexible, you will be lazy with your lead leg action. If you don't have flexibility in the shoulders and arms, you will not be able to go through the full range of motions without tension. When you are flexible, the muscles have been stretched to their extremes, and the chance of pulled muscles is greatly reduced.

Your muscles work in pairs and are known as antagonistic muscles. When one set flexes, the other set relaxes and extends. If you develop one set over the other, you have lost the harmony of action between those antagonistic muscles. Both partners must be fully developed and be able to stretch to their capacity, so that the athlete will have the freedom of motion necessary for top performance.

All the exercises prescribed are related to the specific acts incorporated in the pitching motion. These strengthening exercises will also increase your reflex action and speed as well as developing power.

It takes a great deal of determination and desire to stay with an organized program of exercise. I recognize the fact that these exercises will become very boring and monotonous, but there is no substitute for flexibility and strengthening exercises to ensure success in sports.

Many people believe that a pitcher cannot increase his throwing speed. There are some who don't believe hitting, or even running, can be taught to any large extent. But I know that if you have

the correct mechanics and regularly do strengthening and flexibility exercises, you can increase your
pitching speed, your running speed, and your hitting power.

1. Pre-Spring Training Program, or Winter Program

It is obvious that you must have a pre-spring training program to condition yourself to be ready to hit,
field, throw, and run, run, run during spring training.
The candidate must realize that nobody can get him
ready for the grueling season of baseball but himself, and he cannot wait for the spring training
period to do so. He must start this period of conditioning his mind and body around January 15.

A program of continuous, gradual, progressive
calisthenic exercises must be undertaken. You will
have to put out a great amount of energy and suffer
some pain as you extend your muscles to the extreme.
Remember it takes time to prepare the body, to improve its strength, stamina, endurance, and skill. Start
easy and slowly, increasing the intensity and number
of times performed daily. Soon the muscles will be
able to absorb the punishment of a long, hard workout. Keep pushing the "fatigue barrier" back by increasing the time or repetitions of a specific exercise.

When you arrive at spring training you will be
ready both physically and mentally to tackle the jobs
of hitting, fielding, throwing, and running. You will
make a good impression because you are ready, and
you will not be one of the many injured players in the
training room. You will be on the field, making the
team and learning something new. Some players
report overweight and spend spring training losing
weight rather than trying to increase their skills.
Because they must diet they also enter the season
weak and tired. For the "old pro," it takes longer

for the body to get in shape. The youngster has to be ready to impress in spring training.

Be smart, do not wait for spring training to get in shape. And if you are going from one sport to another, do not think the first sport has put you in condition for the new one.

There are thousands of exercises that are beneficial. I have selected the following ones because I believe they make up a complete and well-rounded program designed specifically for the act of throwing a baseball. When I was pitching I followed this exact program from January 15 till the day I left for spring training. My father, John H. Shaw, compiled it for me. He spent over forty years as a coach and physical-education teacher.

I am not against weight and isometric exercises. Any exercise is better than none. However, the nearer the exercise comes to the actual performance in baseball, the better it is. I lean away from heavy-weight-lifting and isometrics because they are static exercises. I believe it is best to do the various exercises with as much speed of action, as you go through the complete range of motion, as possible.

I suggest you take one week of preliminary exercises before starting to throw. Remember, you have a long way to go, so don't start throwing hard too soon.

Two workouts a day are advisable. In the morning, practice strength-and-flexibility exercises. In the late afternoon, repeat the flexibility exercises and then practice the mechanics of pitching.

I realize that many people may not have the time for this routine because of responsibilities such as school or a job. But if the desire is there, one workout, either at the local YMCA gymnasium or at home, can be fitted into the day's schedule. Make one workout do. Use the strength-and-flexibility exercises and then throw a baseball.

This is also an ideal program to follow to recover from an arm injury.

A. *Jumping Jack*—to warm up the body, increase circulation (P-88A, B)

B. *Head*
  (1) Rotation right and left (P-89A, B)
  (2) Forward and back (P-90A, B)
  (3) Left and right (P-91A, B)

C. *Arms and Shoulders* (A five-pound dumbbell may be used, but not in the beginning.)
  (1) Small circles
    a. Over head (P-92A)
    b. To the side (P-92B)
    c. Arms in front (P-92C)
    d. Arms extended down (P-92D)
  (2) Large circles (P-93A, B, C)
    a. Windmill
  (3) Arm-swinging
    a. Side and upward, arms stiff (P-94A, B)
    b. Forward, across, and back (P-95A, B)
    c. Forward and upward (P-96A, B)
  (4) "Y" position
    a. Bend at waist and swing arms to a "Y" position (P-97A, B)
    b. Bend at waist and swing arms to the sides (P-98A, B)
  (5) Lying on your back
    a. Full arm (P-99A, B)
    b. One-half arm (P-100A, B)

D. *Elbow* (Use five-pound dumbbells; as you progress, you can increase the weight on this exercise.)

Arm extended down, flex arm upward and then rotate hands inward and down (P-101A, B, C, D)

P-88A

P-88B

P-89A

P-89B

P-91A

P-90A

P-90B

P-91B

P-92A

P-92B

P-92C

P-92D

P-93A

P-93B   **P-93C**

P-94A

P-95A

P-94B

P-95B

P-96A

P-96B

P-97A

P-97B

P-98A

P-98B

P-99A

P-99B

P-100A

P-100B

P-101A

P-101B

P-101C

P-101D

P-102

P-103A

P-103B

E. *Hands*
   (1) Flex fingers, preferably with rubber balls
   (2) Stretch finger and forearm muscles (P-102)
F. *Wrist*
   (1) Push off a wall, using fingertips; keep arm straight (P-103A, B)
   (2) Flip a book or weighted disc with elbow on the table or standing (P-104A, B)
G. *Trunk*
   (1) Bend sideward, left and right (P-105A, B)
   (2) Forward and back, hands on hips; keep the back straight when you go forward (P-106A, B)
   (3) Hands on hips, rotate the upper body to the left and to the right (P-107A, B, C)
H. *Knees*
   One-half-knee-bends
I. *Skipping rope*
J. *Wall pulleys*
   (1) Facing pulleys
      a. Flex and extend arms
      b. Arms extended, bring hands over head and down
      c. Arms extended forward at shoulder level, brings arms sideward and backward
      d. Spread feet, arms overhead, bring the arms down between the legs
   (2) *Back to pulleys*
      a. With alternate arms, at sides, pull forward and back
      b. Use swimming motion
      c. Arm bent at elbow, at shoulder level, use pitching motion
      d. Arms sideward at shoulder level, pull forward, touch hands, return
      e. Standing sideward, make pitching motion with full arm swing

130

P-104A   P-104B

P-105A   P-105B   P-106A   P-106B

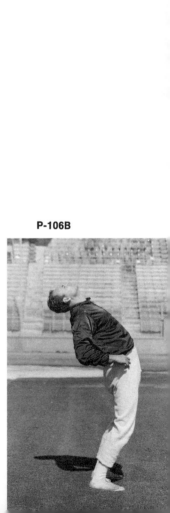

P-107A

P-107B

P-107C

PITCHING

Even though you may be a right-handed pitcher, always do a few *more* exercises for the left side. This is important to keep body symmetry.

K. *Burpees* (P-108A–G)

L. *Flexibility*

   (1) Standing, feet together

      a. Arms extended over head, put palms to floor (P-109A, B)

      b. Grab ankles, try to touch your head to your knees (P-110)

   (2) Standing, feet apart

      a. Assume charge position (P-111)

      b. Grasp ankles, touch head to floor (P-112)

      c. With both hands grasp one ankle, touch head to knee (P-113)

   (3) Sitting position

      a. Soles of feet together, hands to ankles, put head to floor (P-114)

      b. Legs straight, grasp ankles, touch head to knees (P-115)

      c. Legs straight and apart, grasp ankles, touch head to floor (P-116)

      d. Grasp one ankle, touch head to knee (P-117)

   (4) Lying position

      a. With left hand grasp right side of right foot; with right hand push on right knee to straighten out leg (P-118A, B)

      b. Sit up, pull on toes (P-119)

      c. Assume hurdle position (P-120)

M. *Chinning and Hanging*

Start with a few and add one a day to a maximum of 20 pull-ups (P-121A, B)

N. *Sit-ups*

Start with 25 and work up to over 100; bend knees if you wish (P-122A, B)

132

P-108A

P-108B

P-108C

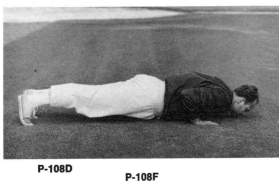

P-108D   **P-108F**

P-108E   **P-108G**

P-109A

P-109B

P-110

P-111

P-112

P-113

P-114

P-115

P-116

P-117

P-118A

P-118B

P-119

P-120

P-121A

P-121B

P-122A

P-122B

O. *Rowing*

Use a rowing machine if you have one

P. *Indian clubs*

Swing the club in a figure eight (P-123)

Q. *Rollers*

(1) Roll up wall, facing wall, all the way to full extension (P-124A, B)

(2) Roll up wall, standing sideward, each arm to full extension (P-125 A, B)

(3) Roll up wall with back to wall (P-126A, B)

(4) Weight on knees, roll to a "Y" (P-127A, B)

R. *Bat-swinging* (P-128) (Add three wraps around the bat each day of any kind of tape.) Swing the bat twenty times with the left hand alone, then twenty times with the right hand alone, then twenty times with both hands. (Swing down on the high ball, level on the belt-high pitch, up on the low ball.) *Always pick a spot on the wall or a spot on the ground to swing at. Learn to control the head of the bat* (P-129A, B, C). Pitchers do not get enough batting practice. This exercise and pepper will help your hitting.

S. *Running*

Run long distances for endurance; in spring training you will run short distances for speed and recovery rate

T. *Swimming*

A good general exercise

Do one more of each exercise each day. Remember, the mediocre athlete quits first. Fatigue of one group of muscles diminishes the amount of work obtainable from another. This is the reason for total body conditioning.

137

P-123   **P-124A**

P-124B

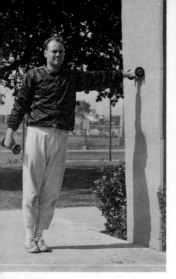

P-125A

P-125B

P-126A

P-126B

P-127A

P-127B

P-128

2. Misconceptions That Still Exist Today

There is an idea that swimming softens the muscles. This is not true. Swimming is an exercise that uses a large number of muscles, especially around the shoulder area. Swimming is a perfect off-season exercise to maintain muscle tone, which is essential in keeping the throwing arm in good shape. After an athlete seriously injures himself, what does the doctor generally recommend? Swimming. So why not swim to reduce the chance of injury and maintain physical well-being?

After a pitcher has had a great year, has worked

139

P-129A

P-129B

P-129C

hard and pitched many innings and made many appearances, many people say, "You've worked hard and you've earned a rest. Take it easy, relax, and rest up." He makes frequent appearances on the banquet circuit, where he is praised continually on the great year he has had. Spring training gets closer and closer, and then he experiences a most unusual thing. He can hardly raise his arm, and when he starts to throw he has nothing on it and may be in tremendous pain. What has happened? It happened to me after the 1959 season, when the Chicago White Sox won the American League pennant. And every year there will be some young pitcher it will happen to who had a great year the season before.

We know that if a leg or arm is in a cast, atrophy sets in almost immediately. I cannot give you a scientific explanation, but if the arm is not used, granules form in the socket and "clicks" are felt when you swing the arm. My advice to the fellow who has had a great year is to *keep using the arm*, whether in golf, swimming, or just some light calisthenics. You will be glad you did. An ounce of prevention is worth a pound of cure.

If you had a bad year, you have to get to work immediately.

Advice not to stretch your muscles because you may pull one is also unfounded. Just the opposite is true; stretch your muscles daily and you will not pull a muscle.

You will hear: "Stop experimenting." Managers and coaches, in my opinion, are often narrow-minded. If you don't experiment and try new things, you will stand still. If you are satisfied with yourself or your record, you will go backward. Remember, the opposition gets to know you. Father Time creeps up on you awfully fast. When you are young and possess a good arm, start with mastery of the fast ball, curve, and change. Don't experiment with odd pitches when you are young, but experiment with grips and so on.

Just because the rosin bag is lying on the mound doesn't mean you have to use it. Most pitchers use it from habit. Some pitching coaches want you to use the rosin bag. Ed Lopat is a big advocate of it. I observed that Early Wynn never used the rosin bag. In fact, he would kick it off the mound. I learned from him that he had a better feel of the ball when he didn't use rosin. Rosin has a slick feeling when it first gets on your hand. Then the body heat melts it and it becomes tacky. Eventually it gets between your fingers and gives you a sticky feeling that I don't like. I personally stopped using rosin and found I had helped my over-all control.

Tip: Never throw on the mound with a rubber or nylon jacket on. Put your jacket on after you throw.

When you do your running in the heat, don't use a rubber jacket while running. You will tire quickly, perspire profusely, and become weak. You will not get a good workout. The fluid you drink after the workout will add the weight you thought you had lost.

When it is cold or windy, a nylon jacket should be worn while running.

Don't drink a lot of water when you are pitching, or you will feel lazy. Guard against this when the weather is hot. Just rinse your mouth out.

XI / The One, Two, Three of Pitching

With runners on base, and especially with a runner on third, the following procedure will save you an occasional moment of embarrassment. A runner can never steal home on you if you use the one, two, three of pitching: (1) Get your sign from the catcher; (2) pick up the runner, look at him; (3) start your motion. Be sure not to move your hand until after you have looked at the runner. Then look home; do not keep looking at the runner. Pick up your target (P-130A, B, C, D).

Many pitchers go one, three, two. They get the sign, start the motion, and then look at the runner. This makes it possible for a real fast runner to steal home. When you look at the runner, he may be try-

P-130A

ing to fake you and be slowly moving toward home. Keep looking at him; sooner or later he will have to stop. When he stops, you can start your motion and pitch. He will never beat the ball home. If he continues to move toward home, step off the rubber and make him get back. If he breaks for home, step back with the right foot and throw home. *With men on base, always remember to step back off the rubber with the right foot before making any moves. You can never balk if you step back off the rubber.*

I have noticed that many pitchers start from a set position with a runner on only third base. I realize they are guarding against the squeeze or stealing home. If you do the one, two, three in that order, the runner can't steal home. The squeeze can still be put on with the pitcher in a set position, because the runner isn't going to take off till your lead foot is about to land, and he can still make it home on a bunt.

I feel you lose that little extra in a set position. I recommend winding up and using the one, two, three of pitching, with a runner on third.

The exception to the rule is when the bases are loaded, with two outs and the count 3–2. Then come to a set position. This keeps the runner on first from scoring on a single.

P-130B

P-130C

P-130D

XII / Who's Covering for the Double Play?

With one or no out and with a runner at first or runners at first and second or runners at first and third, the pitcher should always look to the shortstop or second baseman to see who is covering for the double play in case the ball should be hit back to the pitcher. This should become a habit. Do not throw the ball without knowing who's covering, because when you field the ball you will not have a clear picture of whom you will throw the ball to. Many games have been lost because the pitcher threw the ball away or hesitated before throwing and failed to make the double play.

There are two ways to make the throw to second to start the double play. If the ball is hit sharply and you have caught it and are ready to throw before either the shortstop or second baseman is at the bag, a "bunny hop" or "crow hop" should be taken. This will allow you time to judge the throw and will keep you in motion. The throw to any base must be firm and quick but not extra hard. It is most difficult to handle a ball thrown extra hard; the infielder must be able to handle the ball easily so that he can get it away quickly.

If a ball is hit slow or to the side, you just whirl and throw. Do not take the crow hop. You don't have time.

Always throw with your body under control. Never throw off-balance. Step directly toward the bag.

The ball should be thrown above the belt or chest-high, directly over the bag. The reason the ball is thrown chest-high is that it is easier for the infielder to handle while running full speed. If you threw the ball low, the infielder would have to reach down, maybe lose his balance, and most likely would be unable to recover in time to make the double play. The infielder can see the ball more easily and his hands can work more quickly if it is chest-high.

The bases-loaded double play on a ground ball to the pitcher always goes from the pitcher to the catcher to the first baseman. *Bases loaded, think: home to first.*

Another double play the pitcher takes part in is the ground ball to his left, to the right side of the infield, which takes the first baseman away from the bag. The pitcher gets to first base as quickly as possible, *stops,* gets himself under control, puts his right foot on the bag if he is a right-hander (or his left foot if he is a left-hander), and waits like a first baseman (stretching) for the toss.

The pitcher must make it a habit to break to first on all balls hit to his left. Do not run straight at the bag. Start toward the base path and then come up the line. This will put you in a position to receive the ball at a better angle, and your momentum will not carry you into the runner. The first baseman should try to give the ball to the pitcher as soon as possible. Remember to catch the ball first, then find the bag. Always step toward the center of the diamond and cock your arm immediately, ready to throw home if a runner should attempt to score from second. If the infielder fumbles the ball, get yourself under control and wait for the throw. Do not run by the bag.

XIII / Pick-Off Plays

1. Runner on First

A pitcher should be able to throw in an attempt to pick a runner off first from three positions: when his hands are head-high, when they are halfway down, and from a set position. As you go into your stretch and bring your hands up to your head, the runner starts to take his lead from first base. If the runner used a cross-over leg motion—which a good runner would not use—you would stand a good chance of catching him at this point. Your hands are apart, and you will be able to get the ball to first base very quickly. Don't put the hands together, because you will have to separate them before you can throw and time will be lost. It is also advisable to throw when your hands are on the way down, to keep the runner honest. Your hands are in motion, and you should be able to make a quick snap throw.

Foot action should be quick and it is a reversing action (I-17). When you reverse your feet, the shorter the distance the better. You begin to throw as you turn and throw from your hip. To come overhand is somewhat awkward and takes more time. You should practice throwing the ball on the second-base side of the bag about two feet high, so that the first baseman can make a quick tag.

From a set position there are a number of moves

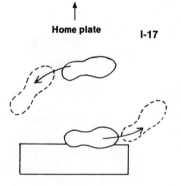

Home plate   I-17

146

that can be used, if they are practiced enough, to keep the baserunner honest. First, let me say that most pitchers reach back to throw to first base. The farther you draw the right hand back, the more time you give the runner to get back. You should make a short, quick throw from the hip. When you open up to throw to first, your throwing hand is already cocked to throw.

Very few pitchers have a good pick-off move, and the reason is simple: very few practice, even in the big leagues. One way to trap the runner is by making a slight quick movement of the shoulder toward home and then coming back and throwing to first. This is generally used by three-quarter-arm pitchers with an open stance. Technically, this is a balk. Any time you deceive the runner, it is a balk. However, if you do it fast and don't exaggerate it, a balk will not be called. Another way, which I believe to be the best, is by quickly putting the weight on the ball of the left foot, forcing the left knee to bend slightly. This gives the illusion of starting to move forward to pitch. You stop the movement with the ball of the left foot and pivot back and throw.

Some pitchers jerk the head up and down or sideways to try to deceive the runner. Actually, all they are doing is rattling their brains. As I said earlier, you must always keep your head up, especially in a set position. In a set position the head turns sidewise to the left to pick up the runner. As you rotate into the pitch, your head will be right on the target with little or no head movement. Any pitcher who lowers his head to look at first base is much easier to steal on. You have to lift your head to throw home. You've given the fast runner another step.

2. How to Stop the Fast Runner

The first thing you want to do is vary the time interval after you get set. You may come down and throw immediately one time; the second time you may stay in a set position as long as five seconds. *Make* the runner stop. Don't be a one-looker. Look once one time, twice another, three times sometimes. Throw over easy one time. Give him your regular pick-off move one time. Then use the pick-off move you have practiced. Also, throw from three positions. These things should help to keep him in his place.

Tip: The first pick-off throw to first that you attempt in a game should be an easy toss. Too many times I have seen the pitcher's first throw be off line and get by the first baseman. However, to be successful in picking off a runner at first or second you must throw the ball hard.

3. Pick-Off Play at First with Runners on First and Second

A complete pitcher should have a pick-off play to first, to second, and to third. A prearranged signal should be established between the pitcher and all his infielders. For example, the infielder may go to his belt buckle and look at the pitcher. Normally, the infielder initiates the play, but the pitcher could start the pick-off play by looking at the infielder and going to his belt buckle. An answer is always given, such as running the hand down the outside of the thigh. This is to ensure that both players know the play is on.

I am a great believer in verbal signals from the infielder to the pitcher for pick-off plays. *A pitcher should automatically look at his infielders between pitches with men on bases to see if a pick-off play is on.* However, during the stress of the game, most pitchers forget to look at the infielder. A verbal sign from the infielder puts the play on, provided the pitcher answers by rubbing his hand down his thigh. An example of a verbal sign might be "Extra"—

"Bob, give him a little extra." Now, without turning around, the pitcher knows the play is on.

With runners on first and second, the first baseman is playing off the base. When the play has been put on, here is how it is executed. The pitcher comes to a set position and looks at second base. While he is looking at second base, he can see the first baseman out of the corner of his right eye (if he is a right-handed pitcher). When the first baseman breaks, the pitcher looks home and throws to first. The timing is almost automatic; actually very little practice is necessary to execute this play correctly. Do not throw the ball too hard. On the other hand, do not "baby" the ball over there. Make a firm throw.

The left-hander executes the play differently. In his case the first baseman doesn't break for the bag till the pitcher starts to lift his lead leg. The left-hander looks at second, picks his leg up, and then steps directly to first. The timing is automatic if the pitcher doesn't rush his throw.

4. Pick-Off at Second

I have heard of many different ways to consummate the pick-off play at second base between the pitcher and the shortstop or second baseman.

The simplest and easiest method to establish co-ordination between the pitcher and infielder is this. The sign is given and answered. The pitcher looks toward second. When the pitcher looks back to home plate, the infielder breaks. The pitcher then whirls and throws. No counting is necessary. The pitcher knows where the infielder is standing and can judge how quickly to whirl and throw. Remember to pause when you look home, then turn and throw.

It has been my experience that the best results in picking a runner off second are achieved without any sign. The play is executed whenever the infielder thinks he has a chance to get the runner. The timing is practically automatic, and very little practice is necessary. Whenever the second baseman or short-stop crosses over with his leg or moves his hand toward second, then you know he is going. The pitcher looks home, turns, and throws to second base. A right-hander turns to his left, a left-hander to his right, when throwing to second base. If the shortstop or second baseman is shuffling to decoy the runner, you know he is not going. I prefer this to the "daylight" play, because it is easier to execute and you don't have to wait till the infielder passes the runner and shows daylight. The throw should be knee-high over the third-base side of second base.

Remember, on any throw to second or third you don't have to throw the ball, so if you don't have a chance to get the runner, don't throw.

5. Pick-Off at Third

This play may be used only once or twice a year, but the pitcher who tries it will more than likely be successful. The third baseman takes his normal position. The play will be used with runners on first and third only. The pitcher comes set, looks at home plate, and as soon as he raises his leg, the third baseman breaks and the pitcher, instead of stepping home, steps toward third and throws the ball to the third baseman before he gets to third. Simply lead the third baseman. Don't wait for him to get to third before giving him the ball. The left-hander works this play by looking for the third baseman to break after he comes set; then he throws to third base.

6. Pick-Off at First by the Left-Handed Pitcher

It is typical of the left-hander to give away his movement in advance by the motion of his head. Many left-handers look at the runner as they lift the lead leg, and then pitch home. The same pitcher will look home when he lifts his lead leg, and throw to first. Maury Wills, a great base-stealer, has mentioned in lectures that this is the most common fault of left-handers.

There are three methods by which a left-hander can pick a runner off first. Warren Spahn had the finest pick-off move to first of any left-hander I have seen. The most important part of the pick-off move by the left-hander is the proper head movement. First, the eyes focus and look straight at the runner —look him in the eye. Second, the leg is picked up; you are still looking at the runner. Third, you look home. Fourth, you step between first and home plate, and look back to first just as you release the ball. Experience has shown me that the Spahn method is difficult for some to master.

The second way is simply to look at the runner, whether you throw to first or home, when you lift your lead leg.

In the third way, look halfway between first base and home plate. This method can prove very deceptive. The baserunner has to wait to see which way you are going when you lift your leg. Very little head movement occurs, adding to deceptiveness.

Two important tips: Step with the lead leg between home and first. You do not have to step directly toward first. The weight should slide toward home. Don't throw overhand. Throw from the side.

The following is an offensive play used primarily against a left-handed pitcher in a set position with runners on first and third and usually with two outs

151

and a weak hitter at the plate. The offensive team may try to steal a run by having the runner on third break as soon as the pitcher brings his hands up, going into his set position. The runner on first breaks for second as soon as he sees the runner at third head for home. If the pitcher throws to first, it is impossible to get the runner at home. Some pitchers will balk, or if they hesitate momentarily the runner on third will score. To prevent the score, the left-hander must know exactly what to do. Step back off the rubber and pick up the lead runner, who is the man on third (the important run). When you see him running, throw home. If the runner isn't far off third base, get the ball to the second baseman or shortstop as quickly as possible.

7. Pick-Off at Second with Bases Loaded or Runners on Second and Third

When the pitcher is in a windup position, looking at the catcher, and the shortstop or second baseman thinks he can pick off the runner at second, he gives the sign to the catcher—glove to right elbow, or whatever the sign may be. The catcher then gives the same sign to the pitcher and taps the inside of his right or left thigh, to tell the pitcher whether the shortstop or second baseman is covering on the pick-off play.

The catcher gives the normal signs to the pitcher and then gets into his catching stance, watching and waiting for the infielder to break for second base.

When the infielder breaks, the catcher drops his glove sharply, which tells the pitcher to whirl and throw to second base.

XIV / How to Execute
Fielding Plays

The suggested position of the hands when you are fielding a ground ball is right hand on top of left. Also spread your feet, get your butt down, and reach out with your hands (P-131).

1. Defense against the Bunt Situation

With a runner on first, when the bunt is in order, the pitcher should move straight in quickly. If the ball is bunted back to him he should rotate counterclockwise and throw to second base without delay. The first baseman will be charging on his left, the third baseman on his right, so the pitcher must move straight in quickly.

With a runner on first in a bunt situation in the later part of the game, it is critical to stop the runner from advancing to second base. The first baseman must hold the runner at first base and charge for home when the pitcher starts his delivery. (You bunt to first with a runner on first because the first baseman has to hold the runner on.) Here is a defensive play to stop the runner from advancing to second base.

The manager can give the sign to the first baseman. The play is used only in a close game, and in the

P-131

later part of the game. To avoid confusion the first baseman should jog to the mound to tell the pitcher that he is going to charge—"Don't throw over," or "Throw over once; then I'll charge," or "Throw over twice; then I'll charge." The pitcher doesn't throw to first when the first baseman is charging. He sees the first baseman out of the corner of his eye. He waits, giving the first baseman a couple of strides toward home, then throws home. This gives the first baseman time to field the ball and throw the runner out at second base.

There are four defensive plays against the bunt situation with runners on first and second or just on second.

(a) With runners on first and second or a runner just on second, when the bunt is in order, the pitcher breaks toward the third-base side of the infield. This is because the third baseman has to hold his position. If the ball is bunted hard toward third, he will come in, field the ball, and throw to first. No play can be made on the runner going to third. The offensive team has executed the play properly. The reason the pitcher breaks to third is that this is where the ball should be bunted. If the pitcher is able to get to the ball quickly enough, the illustration shows the proper way to execute the play (P-132A, B). Fielding and throwing of the ball should be one motion, if possible. The pitcher should not raise his body up to make this play and should throw from the side. Try to position yourself correctly, as in the illustration,

P-132A

P-132B

to make it easier to rotate counterclockwise when throwing to third. Left-handers, of course, don't have to turn when throwing to third. This play (number one) is always on unless the catcher signals one of the other three plays.

(*b*) With runners on first and second with a two-run lead in the later part of a game, the manager may want to put on this play, especially if there is a slow runner on first. The third baseman charges on this play, with the pitcher and the first baseman. The shortstop goes to second, and the second baseman to first. The object is to stop the tying runner from going to second. This is play number two.

(*c*) The objective in play number three is to stop the runner on second base from reaching third on a bunt. The shortstop comes in behind the runner, then breaks for third. The pitcher gives the shortstop a couple of steps before he delivers the ball home. Third baseman, pitcher, and first baseman charge and throw the ball to the shortstop at third. The second baseman goes to first.

(*d*) Play number four is a pick-off at second base. The shortstop comes in behind the runner at second base and breaks, letting the runner see him start toward third. The second baseman breaks to second when the pitcher looks home. The pitcher pauses and throws to second, attempting to pick off the runner. The catcher gives the sign for all these plays.

2. Backing Up the Bases

Another responsibility of the pitcher is to back up the bases. A general rule to follow is always to back up the base ahead of the runner. In other words, if the runner's coming to second, you back up third. If the runner's coming into third, you back up home. There is one play that will add some confusion. This is when the runner is going to second and you don't know for sure if the play will be at third or home plate. The best thing to do is to go halfway between home and third base. As the play develops you can make your move to back up the base that the play calls for. Remember this: *You want to be backing up the base where there might be a play on the runner.*

Always remember to get far enough behind the base so that if the ball is deflected from the infielder you will be in a position to move forward, picking up the ball, so that you have the play in front of you. If you have to run backward to get the ball, the runner will more than likely be able to take the next base.

There are two plays where the pitcher is cut-off man. The first is when *runners are on first and third* and a short fly ball is hit down the first-base line or third-base line. If it goes down the right-field line, fair or foul, right fielder, first baseman, and second baseman go for the ball. You, the pitcher, should run toward first base and line up with third base. If you do, then neither player can advance. If you stay on the mound or back up home, one baserunner can advance, and you can't stop the play. For example, if any of the fielders down the line catches the ball with the pitcher behind home or still on the mound, the runners have both tagged up on the play and will break. If the throw goes to second, the runner stops and the run scores from third. Two long throws will never get the runner on third. If the throw goes home to get the runner from third, he simply stops and goes back to third, while the runner on first moves to second. There is nobody to cut off the ball, and it goes home. Two long throws will never get the runner on first. It's the same with a short fly ball down the third-base line. The pitcher goes directly toward the second-base side of third base.

In the second play, with *runners on first and second or bases loaded,* a ground ball is hit between the first baseman and second baseman. Both go for the ball. The pitcher is cut-off man on the throw from the right fielder. On all other plays the pitcher backs up third or home.

The pitcher should cover home on a wild pitch or a ball that gets away from a catcher with any runners on base.

It is essential for the pitcher to help out on any pop-ups between home and first or home and third. The infielder and catcher will be running at each other with their heads up. The pitcher should run over to the foul line or farther and shout loud, and more than once, the name of the man who, in his judgment, can catch the ball more easily. Remember, a fielder can generally catch the ball more easily. First, he has a fielder's glove on. Second, he doesn't have a lot of gear on. Third, the ball will be curving toward him. A ball hit off the bat always curves toward the infield. Do not call the play too quickly.

When a pitcher has the ball and sees a runner stop between the bases, he should run at him, but always force the runner to go back to the base he came from or the one away from home plate. He should have his arm cocked so he can throw quickly if he needs to.

XV / Pitcher-Catcher Relationship

There must be a smooth working relationship between the pitcher and the catcher. There should be a meeting of the minds before each game, when the weakness and strength of each hitter are reviewed and signals and switches are agreed upon.

A young pitcher would do well to listen to an experienced catcher and take his advice, but as time goes on the pitcher must assume the responsibility of the pitch and not depend entirely on the judgment of the catcher. There is no guarantee that the catcher is a permanent member of the team; he may be traded or injured.

Do not hesitate, when you have gained experience, to have the confidence to pitch what you want, not what the catcher wants. The final judgment is yours.

Communication between the pitcher and the catcher is by signs. The sign language should be simple, direct, and easy to understand. It is of paramount importance that the pitcher develop his own set of signs and switches.

In the big leagues, binoculars, telescopes in the scoreboard, television, and many other ingenious ways of getting the signs from the catcher have been used. If the other team got the signs the day before, it is imperative that you have your own set of signs,

158

different from anyone else's. Some managers in the big leagues want everyone on their pitching staff to use the same set of signs. I disagree with this system emphatically, because if the opposition gets one set, it has them all. I admit it is easier for the infielders to get used to one set of signs. But if the opposition gets your signs it won't matter whether the infielders know what's coming or not. Besides, it doesn't take long for an infielder or catcher to learn your particular set of signs.

There are many different sets of signs, but switches must be a part of them. Keep in mind that there are hundreds of different sets or types of signs that can be devised. Let's assume that one finger is the fast ball; two, the curve; three, the slider; four, the change. Let me give you a typical system of signs, using outs as the key (scoreboard signs). The catcher should give a sequence of three signs to the pitcher, whether there are men on base or not. You may use the first sign with no outs, the second sign with one out, and the third sign with two outs. Or you might use the first sign with no strikes, the second sign with one strike, and the third sign with two strikes. These are just two examples. The glove of the catcher can be used to give signs, the position of his head, what he touches, various sequences of fingers. There are pump signs and many others, too numerous to mention.

The next important thing is that the catcher have a switch. This switch would apply only to the next pitch. As an example, if the catcher touched his left shoulder with his throwing hand, it would be the first sign. If he touched his left elbow, it would be the second sign. If he touched his wrist it would be the third sign. If we were using outs as the key and there were two outs, he would normally use the third sign given. But if the catcher touched his shoulder it would be the first sign for just that pitch. Then you revert back to your regular set of signs.

So far we have established that we must have basic sets of signs and the catcher must have a switch. I might add that the pitcher always nods his head to acknowledge to the catcher that he has seen the switch for that pitch. Third, the pitcher should have a switch. If the catcher calls for a fast ball and the pitcher wants to throw a curve ball, it makes little sense to have the catcher go through a whole group of signs again. He might call for a change-up, and the pitcher will shake his head again, and the whole process will start all over again. Neither one will look as if he knows what he is doing, confusion reigns, and the fans get tired of waiting. So if the pitcher has a simple switch, like rubbing his glove hand down his leg, that switches the fast ball to the breaking ball and the breaking ball to the fast ball. If the catcher gives the pitcher a fast-ball sign when the pitcher wants to throw a change-up, no sign is necessary because it won't throw the catcher off if he throws the change off the fast ball. If the catcher calls for a fast ball and the pitcher rubs his glove down his left leg, the catcher looks for a curve ball. If the pitcher wants to throw a slow curve, the catcher will be able to handle it without any problem because he is looking for a hard curve. If a pitcher has a slider and a curve, the catcher would look for the slider, not the curve, when the pitcher switches from the fast ball, because the curve is slower and can be handled easily if you are looking for a slider.

A pitcher should never start the preliminary motion until the catcher has shown where he wants the pitch thrown. Before or after he has given the sign, the catcher should tap the inside of his left thigh or his right thigh, to show where he wants the ball thrown. He should tap twice if he wants the pitch off the plate for a ball. If the catcher wants a fast ball inside and the pitcher wants to throw outside, the simplest way to tell him is by shaking the head. The catcher will know that the pitcher wants to throw to the other side. The pitcher uses the left hand (glove hand) to switch the pitch and uses his head to indicate where he wants to throw it.

A pitcher can also control both what he throws and where he throws it, with his head. For instance, if the catcher calls for a fast ball and the pitcher shakes his head, the catcher should follow a definite sequence to avoid spending unnecessary time. He will put down two fingers for a curve. If the pitcher shakes his head again, the catcher will put down three fingers for slider, and so on. He should not jump around and break the sequence. Then he signals "inside" by tapping the inside of his left thigh if a right-handed hitter is up. If the pitcher shakes his head, the catcher knows that he wants it outside.

Another method of switching pitches, which Juan Marichal uses, is to rub once or twice above the belt to add, and below the belt to subtract. For example, if one is a fast ball, two is a curve, three is a slider, four is a change. The catcher calls for number one, and the pitcher rubs his chest twice, meaning "add two." So the pitcher will throw the slider. If the catcher called for number one and the pitcher rubbed once below the belt, he would throw the change-up.

If you want to be a pitcher who is in control of the situation, and if you truly want a good pitcher-catcher relationship, I recommend that you have a close association with the catcher. Warm up with him as much as possible, so he can learn what pitches you like to throw in certain situations. The closer you work together, the closer your thinking will be.

Keep in mind that switching just to switch is silly. Always have a reason for throwing a certain pitch.

If the catcher keeps putting the glove right down the middle, the pitcher should request that he give a lower target or move it in or out. In the lower minors especially, when a catcher isn't experienced or is worrying about a runner on base, he will give a target that is convenient to him and will put him in an easy position to throw a potential runner out. The pitcher's eyes will instinctively pick up the glove, and more than likely he will hit it. If the target is right in the middle of the strike zone, the hitter stands a good chance to hit the pitcher hard.

Every pitcher has started his motion with a divided mind many times and wishes he hadn't. For example, the catcher puts his glove inside and low, and you want to throw low and away. You start your motion thinking outside and looking inside. Being undecided, you end up throwing down the middle without your usual good stuff. Once you make a decision, go through with it. *Don't be indecisive.*

When a pitcher shakes a catcher's sign off, he is thinking and is making progress in most instances.

A pitcher should know where his catcher likes the pitch-out thrown. Generally the ball is thrown about two and a half feet off the plate, opposite the batter, above the belt so the hitter can't hit the ball and the catcher can get rid of the ball quickly.

On an intentional walk, the catcher will stand up and put his glove or hand out to the side to indicate where he wants the ball thrown. The pitcher should come to a set position, check the runner, and throw the ball firmly, but not hard, about four or five feet outside. This gives the catcher time to get out that far and catch the ball.

XVI / Pitcher-Umpire Relationship

In the ideal situation the catcher handles any questionable calls of balls or strikes.

He is in a better position to judge the pitch than the pitcher is. When a pitcher comes off the mound violently, his head moves, and it is sometimes difficult to judge whether the pitch did cross the plate.

A catcher should never argue with an umpire unless he is positive he is right. The pitcher should always ask his catcher if it was a ball or a strike first, before showing any disapproval of the umpire's decision.

Many pitchers get themselves emotionally worked up to such a state that it affects their pitching. As a general rule, it is best to show no emotion on the mound and say nothing to the umpire. If you must express disapproval, be an actor. Act the part, but do not become emotionally involved, for if you do you will not be able to concentrate on the job of pitching. I have never known an umpire to change a ball or strike decision. If you get a raw deal, forget it. During the season the good and bad calls will even out.

Umpires are human beings with feelings, trying to do the best they can. They make mistakes, and so do you. Pitchers who constantly complain and argue seldom get the close pitch.

If you must object to the umpire, say what you've got to say—don't make a big scene—return to the mound, and continue pitching.

163

XVII / Hitters' Weaknesses

It is important for a young pitcher to know the fundamentals of hitting so that he can determine the various weaknesses of the opposing hitters. Here are some specific things to look for when you observe a hitter.

Let's start with the hitter's feet. The feet should be comfortably apart, approximately shoulder width. A hitter who has his feet close together will generally have to take a long stride. As a rule you can change speeds on this type of hitter. The opposite is true for a hitter with a wide stance. Generally speaking, the hitter with a wide stance is harder to change up on.

The position of the feet should be noticed. If the toes are pointed out, the hitter will probably restrict his hips. If the right-handed hitter doesn't point the left toe toward the pitcher, he is locking his front hip and is more of a straight-away hitter than a pull hitter. The foot position for hitting is about the same as the foot position in golf. The back foot should be perpendicular to the pitcher, and the toe of the front foot should point slightly toward the pitcher.

Does the hitter have a closed, open, or square stance? Actually, the stance makes no difference, providing the hitter steps correctly, straight ahead toward the pitcher, and keeps the lead shoulder closed. How a hitter starts is not important; it's the position he gets to when he is about to swing that counts. Observe where the hitter steps. As a general rule, the direction in which the lead foot steps determines where the hitter's power is. For example, if the hitter steps in toward the plate, he probably will hit to the opposite field well but can be jammed rather easily. If the hitter steps away from the plate, he is more inclined to pull and he can be pitched away.

After you have checked the stride of the hitter, it is most important to see if he covers the entire plate with his bat after he strides. For example, if he is up close to the plate and steps away and still has the plate covered with the bat, he is in the correct position. You are looking for the hitter who steps away and doesn't cover the outside portion of the plate. You can get him out on balls away.

Watch and see where the hitter stands in the batter's box. The farther back in the box he stands, the harder it will be for him to hit the breaking pitch. Most good breaking-ball hitters more or less straddle the plate. Specifically, the lead foot is up to the front edge of the plate.

Most hitters will give their weaknesses away. (I am, of course, speaking in generalities.) If a man is close to the plate, he probably has trouble with the ball away; that is why he is up on the plate. The opposite is also true.

Check the hitter's arms when he swings at the ball away and the ball inside. The arms are extended on the ball away, but the lead arm bends and the hands come in, in order to handle the ball inside. The hitter who always extends his arms will have trouble inside. The quick bat generally separates the good hitter from the bad hitter. The hitter with the slow bat, or a hitter who sweeps the bat, will have trouble with the ball inside (jam him).

If you haven't seen a hitter before, what may tip off whether he is a low- or high-ball hitter is the way in which he takes his preliminary swing. This is not always true, but it is the case more often than not. Watch how he swings the bat before he gets into the batter's box. Some hitters swing up, indicating they are low-ball hitters, and some swing down, indicating they may be high-ball hitters.

Watch the hands. They should move back and up as the foot strides forward. If the hitter drops his hands, it is almost a certainty that he will not be able to handle a high pitch. He will have a tendency to uppercut the ball or be late on the good fast ball. The correct way to hit the high pitch is to hit down on it. The head of the bat should be above the hands. Most hitters who have the back elbow sticking up, which causes the head of the bat to point straight up, have a tendency to loop the bat and generally swing up on the ball. When you see a hitter do this, he is probably dropping his back shoulder. This indicates that he will have trouble with the high ball. The elbow of the back arm should be pointing at the ground, not at the horizon.

Some hitters exaggerate hitting down on the ball to such an extent that they are good high-ball hitters but fail to swing properly on the low ball. The bat can be swung level only on the ball about belt-high. You swing down on the high ball, head of the bat above the hands; and up on the low ball, head of the bat below the hands. Keep in mind that if the batter exaggerates hitting down on the ball he will hit ground balls. The home-run "power hitter" has a tendency to swing on a slightly upward plane to put the ball in the air. As a general rule, there are few good low-ball hitters. For some reason more of them are left-handed than right-handed hitters.

Generally speaking, the pull hitter, the fellow who

is trying to hit the home run, will find it difficult to handle the low outside pitch. Remember that you will get hurt more on the inside half of the plate than on the outside half. Whenever you are in doubt, the safest thing to do is pitch low and away, especially in this day and age, when everyone is trying to hit the ball out of the park.

Watch to see if the head pulls or jerks away, and if the lead shoulder pulls away. If they do, you can pitch down and away with the fast ball, and the hitter will have difficulty hitting the curve.

Do the wrists roll too soon? If they do, the head of the bat will come up and over rather than stay on one plane, making it very difficult to hit the curve. Batters who do this are generally pull hitters. Keep the ball down and away.

With regard to the hit and run, it has been my experience in the big leagues that the outstanding hit-and-run men can handle the inside pitch better than the ball down and away. This is definitely opposite to what you might expect or have been taught.

A good time to start to learn about your adversary is during batting practice. Watch every move a hitter makes. Try to get as close to the batting cage as possible. Sometimes a hitter will tell you his weaknesses. If he's smart, he will be working on them. You may hear him say to the batting-practice pitcher, "Throw me balls away," or "Sliders inside." Try to learn the hitter's mental make-up. If he is a big RBI man, he will want to drive in the run from second. He may go after bad balls if he is the type who is overanxious to drive a run in. You may not have to throw him a good strike, even though you are two balls and no strikes. He definitely doesn't want to walk, and more likely he will swing at a borderline pitch.

A pitcher should learn everything about the mechanics and fundamentals of hitting. I get a big chuckle out of my fellow professionals who make their living as hitters; they think that all pitchers are completely ignorant about hitting. But to be an outstanding pitcher you must know all about it.

Concentrate, observe, study, and analyze your opponents' hitting techniques, and do yourself a favor —keep a book. Gather information. Ask pitchers on other teams how they pitch to certain hitters. Confer with your fellow players and manager.

XVIII / Pitching Strategy

1. How to Set Up the Hitter

What do we mean when we say "Set up the hitter"? You have observed, studied, and examined the statistics and abilities of the opposing hitter. You have come to certain conclusions regarding his strengths and weaknesses. You also take into consideration other pertinent facts: the ball park, the wind, the defensive abilities of your teammates, and the score of the game. You know your own strengths and weaknesses. Do not forget the element of surprise. Setting up the hitter means taking advantage of all these things.

First let me say that it is easier to talk about setting up a hitter than it is to do it. This is one department that is governed by your ability, control, and mental make-up. Pitching strategy is complex and changes constantly, for every hitter and situation. There are, however, a number of basic ideas that will help you because they have proved successful in the past.

The first pitch to the hitter, no matter what specific pitch you throw, should be a strike.

I believe you can throw your fast ball on the first pitch the first time you face any hitter and have the percentages in your favor. You are strong at the beginning of a game. The hitter may not be sure where you will release the ball. He doesn't know how

169

hard you are throwing. He doesn't know how much the ball is moving. This doesn't hold true after you have faced him two or three times. He has been able to study you and has gauged your fast ball; therefore the percentages are no longer in your favor.

Assuming you have mastered the mechanics and therefore possess control, as I have said previously, *never give in to the hitter*. In other words, don't throw the ball down the middle in a given situation.

Always get ahead of the hitter. If you get the first strike, you have the hitter at a distinct disadvantage. You now have two chances to nick a corner. If you succeed in nicking the corner, or get the hitter to swing at a borderline pitch, you have a count of 0–2. Now you have three chances to nick the corner. If the count is 2–1, you are actually even with the hitter. Don't say to yourself, "I must throw a strike," putting yourself on the defensive mentally; you will end up giving in to the hitter by throwing the ball down "death valley." Think positively. If you have missed the corner on the last two pitches, the percentages are that you will nick the corner on the third pitch. Don't plant negative thoughts. The mind controls the body.

Let's assume you have thrown a ball and the count is 3–1. The hitter stands in the batter's box with one thing on his mind: "I've got the pitcher where I want him." A little egotism creeps into his thoughts, and he is sure that a big fat fast ball will be coming his way. Now is the time to throw the change of pace, slider, or curve. If you want to throw the fast ball— depending upon the hitter—keep it down or have an idea where you are going to throw the ball. Again I say don't give in to the hitter and throw the ball down the middle. What does the manager tell the power hitter to do on 3–1 and 3–0? "If it's a nice, big, fat, juicy pitch, let her go." I see no reason why we should accommodate the hitter and give him just that.

Is a pitcher hurt more on a high pitch or on a low pitch? On a high pitch.

Is a pitcher hurt more on a pitch inside or outside? Inside. The low outside pitch, in this day and age with the lively ball and the thin-handled bats, is probably best when you're not sure or you don't want to get hurt by the long ball.

Remember to keep the ball low.

The expression "Pitch to the L" was taught to me by Lew Burdette. The illustration (I-18) best describes this theory. Try to throw to the "heavy line."

Remember that there are many first-ball hitters. Learn who they are.

Remember there is no rule to say you cannot repeat the same pitch three or four, or possibly five, times in a row. There are also times when a change-up can be followed with another change.

I-18

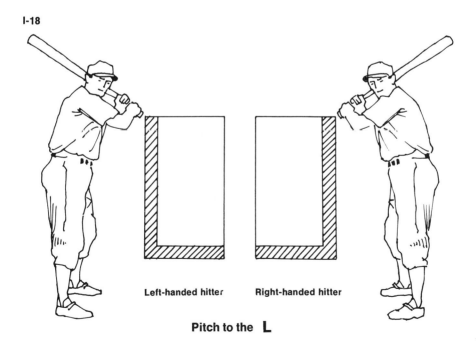

Left-handed hitter   Right-handed hitter

Pitch to the L

In my experience, a good pitch with the count 0–2 is a fast ball, with your best stuff, low and away. Attempt either to "nick" or miss the corner. You will often get a called strike.

When you decide to pitch up and in or move the hitter back, don't let a vision of the hitter creep into your mind, causing you unconsciously to ease up on the pitch. This is a natural tendency, but you must guard against it. To avoid it, aim at his hands.

Never lose confidence in your fast ball. An older pitcher should remember this particularly. Everything works off the fast ball.

Young pitchers, especially, often make the mistake of giving in to the hitter with a runner on second or third and first base open. Remember that the game can be lost in the early innings just as easily as in the later innings. Look over and see who the on-deck hitter is. Remember if you end up walking the hitter you set up a double-play situation if there are fewer than two outs.

When your team takes the lead, especially in the late innings of a game, victory is in your grasp and your heart may beat a little faster. Learn to relax and concentrate on the job at hand, which is to get each hitter out as he comes up. The best suggestion I have is to go to the mound and make believe it is a 0–0 ballgame.

Many managers tell a pitcher, after his team takes the lead, to "throw strikes." The manager, by making this statement, actually adds more pressure to the situation. If the pitcher should throw a ball on the first pitch, he starts thinking only of throwing strikes. Negative thoughts creep into his mind; he may tense up, and his concentration on getting the hitter out is broken.

It is true that when you have a lead you should

try not to walk anybody. Many inexperienced pitchers go exclusively to the fast ball. Don't change your style of pitching, which has been successful up to this point. Continue to mix your pitches and change speeds. Your style is probably why you're winning at this stage of the game.

When you have a substantial lead and you get behind in the count, by all means throw the pitch you have best command of, which is generally the fast ball. *Make the batter earn his way on.*

Remember, most managers have the batter take one strike before they allow him to swing, during the last two or three innings, if his team is down by three or more runs. Take advantage of this fact and get ahead of the hitter with your fast ball. The opposition will let you know quickly if they are taking the first strike. On the other hand, if they are jumping on the first pitch, change your strategy and mix up your pitches.

The manager will not put on the take in a close ball game with a runner in scoring position, and remember that the hitter is anxious to swing to drive in the runner. If you get behind in the count and come in with a fast ball to get a strike down the middle, you increase the chances of a base hit. If you walk the hitter, you set up a double-play situation. If there is one out, you can get out of the inning with one pitch. *Don't give in to the hitter.*

2. Quick Pitch

Occasionally it may be appropriate to catch a hitter unawares by changing your normal delivery. For example, you always bring your hands over your head in the preliminary motion. For a quick pitch you can simply put your hands together in front of your belt and throw with no preliminary motion. Unless

173

P-133A

P-133B

P-133C

the umpire has called time or has his hand up, it is a legal pitch.

The same can be done in a set position, but you must be careful to pause with your hands together for a "full second" or a balk will be called (P-133A, B, C).

3. Pitching in a Bunt Situation

Most coaches have been saying, "In a bunt situation throw your fast ball up," for so long that it is an accepted truth. I disagree with it for a number of reasons. I conducted an experiment over a period of years and proved to myself that the hardest ball to bunt is a fast curve low and away or a fast ball low and away.

The coach says to use the fast ball and get it up because he hopes for a little pop-up. In my opinion, if the bunter does not hold the bat level but holds it with the right hand above and ahead of the left (if he is a right-handed hitter), he reduces the chances of popping the ball up. In other words, he uses "bat angle." (Some organizations teach "bat angle" and some teach "keep the bat parallel to the ground.") In my experiments the fast ball was bunted successfully more often up than down, and more often on the inside of the plate than away. The low fast curve or slider was bunted least successfully. Many veteran pitchers will throw the fast ball up and in, in a bunt situation. The bunter tries to get out of the way of the pitch and instinctively raises his hands and often fouls the ball off.

Let's assume the bunt has been taken off and you come in with a high fast ball. This is exactly what and where the hitter will be looking for it, and the chances of getting hit hard are good.

The most important thing to remember in a bunt

174

situation is to throw the ball hard. Velocity on your fast ball is important.

Another reason I don't believe in starting a hitter off high is that you can get yourself behind in the count if he takes it. Many times a pitcher who is trying to keep the hitter from bunting the ball ends up walking him.

If you are ahead in the count and the batter does bunt with a level bat, then you might try pitching him high, hoping for a pop-up. If you observe a bunter using "bat angle," then I suggest pitching him down.

How can you find out if the hitter is going to bunt? Come to a set position. Hold it a second or two and then step back quickly with your right foot. Watch the hitter as you do it. He will move slightly, giving the bunt away. Step back on, quickly, and pitch.

If a pitcher tries this on you while you are hitting, step out of the batter's box and look at the third-base coach. The pitcher then has to revamp his thinking and ask himself if the third-base coach has changed the sign.

4. Daily Program

If you are a starting pitcher, you should have a regular program for the days between starts, whether you are in a four-day or a five-day rotation. The first day after you pitch, you will probably be stiff and sore. If you won, you will enjoy working hard. If you lost, you had better work extra hard for two reasons: to build yourself up mentally and so as not to radiate a defeatist attitude to the rest of the club. Begin preparing yourself for your next start. If you are in a four-day rotation, do your flexibility exercises. Play at least fifteen minutes of pepper. Run—fifteen or more 60-yard sprints. The more work you do the first day, the sooner the stiffness will leave. Second day: flexibility exercises, pepper, throw to a catcher on the sidelines, then run. This is your day for a good workout. Third day: flexibility exercises, a little pepper—five or ten minutes—no throwing, little running (just loosen up and get a sweat). Fourth day: pitch.

If you are in a five-day rotation, your first day will be the same. Second day: plenty of flexibility exercises and pepper. You can either throw to a catcher or throw batting practice. If you do, don't throw very hard or very long—approximately ten or fifteen minutes. Run—get a good workout. Third day: flexibility exercises and pepper; throw to a catcher; have a good loosening-up session. Run. Fourth day: a few flexibility exercises, some pepper, a little running. Take it easy this day. Fifth day: pitch.

Relief pitchers usually do the same thing each day. There is a slight difference between the "short man" and the "long man." The short man is usually used only during the seventh, eighth, and ninth innings. The long man can be used any time from the first inning through the sixth as a general rule. Both long men and short men should do flexibility exercises, play pepper, and run (at least ten 60-yard sprints).

Of course several factors determine how much running is advisable—such as how much pitching you are doing, frequency of appearances, and climatic conditions such as heat.

Most outstanding pitchers work hard.

A manager can help a pitcher by telling him in advance whether he is a starter, long man, or short man. Then he will know how much to work out before the game.

Johnny Sain advocates a different daily program, which I feel has much merit, and that is to throw *every day*. Whitey Ford of the New York Yankees followed it one year and won over twenty ball games. I followed it one year with the San Francisco Giants and had one of my best years. It includes throwing the day after you pitch a nine-inning ball game. You do not throw hard but simply loosen up. The sooner you throw, the sooner the stiffness goes away. The other advantages are that you keep the feel of the ball and practice your delivery and control and continue to work on your various pitches, spin, et cetera. These daily workouts are not long and *you do not throw hard.* Infielders and outfielders warm up every day. The pitcher can do the same thing only on the mound.

5. Starting versus Bullpen

Each individual will find through experience his best method for warming up as a starter. However, this is the general procedure of most major-league pitchers.

How much time will you use to warm up? The first thing to take into consideration is the weather, or, more specifically, the temperature. On hot days in midsummer you will require only ten minutes to get ready. On a cold day, fifteen minutes or more will be needed. (The weight of your undershirt—light or heavy—will be governed by the temperature. The sleeve should cover the elbow.)

Should you warm up near home plate or in the bullpen? I suggest throwing in the bullpen for two reasons. First, the mound in the bullpen is similar to the one you will be working on during the game; the one near home plate is flat. Second, the opposition is farther away and can't study you as well.

Let me suggest that you have yourself all set, dressed, and in the dugout, at least five minutes before the time you will start warming up. Don't make anybody go looking for you, and don't make a frantic run from the clubhouse to start warming up. Managers like to see an organized pitcher. Another suggestion: know ahead of time who will warm you up, and tell him when you want to start.

As I have said, it is important before each game to go over with your catcher how you will pitch each hitter. It is best for each of you to know what the other is thinking so you can work together efficiently. Some managers hold meetings and some don't. There is no rule that says you can't tell your infielders or outfielders how you will pitch a hitter.

If you are on the home team, you will be going to the mound first, so complete your warm-up in time to dry yourself off with a towel; go to the john if necessary, rinse your mouth out with water, and take a breather. I wanted to be on the mound for the National Anthem. Some stay in the dugout and relax in the back and then come out and start their warm-up throws. I liked to get there early so I could get a few extra warm-up tosses.

The days of "pacing yourself" as a starter are gone. The theory "Go as hard as you can as long as you can" has proved to be correct. Don't save yourself; it might be too late and you could end up in the shower feeling strong after the relief pitcher has taken your place.

If you pitch often enough you will get knocked out. Let's hope it doesn't happen often, and if it does there will be a reason for it. However, when it happens, the world has not come to an end. Don't get excited, don't make excuses, don't blame other players, and above all don't blame the manager for taking you out. Don't throw your glove—as we all have done. Sit down and try to figure what you are doing wrong, what mistakes you have made.

I suggest, if you are going to remain on the bench, that you change your undershirt to avoid a chill.

Usually everyone has seen enough of you and the logical thing to do is go in and get out of your wet uniform and take a shower. Get dressed and go into the stands and watch the remainder of the game.

When you start to warm up before the game, throw easy. Always warm up on the rubber. Your catcher should start near you and move back as you loosen up. The pitcher needs the feel of working off the rubber. Use your full windup as you would in a game, to practice the correct groove. *Don't start in front of the rubber as a starter or—especially—as a reliever.*

As you warm up, you will start with your fast ball, but don't keep throwing mostly fast balls. This is a mistake made by many pitchers. Go to the curve and slider and mix in your change-up from a windup position. *Be sure the catcher moves the target in and out* and occasionally up and down. Don't throw the curve hard when you start throwing it. Start easy and build up.

After you are fairly loose, go to a set position and then throw all your pitches, concentrating on the target as usual. After you have completed your warm-ups in a set position, go back to your windup and make believe you are pitching to a specific hitter. This helps to prepare you mentally for the game.

I opened up and threw hard for about ten pitches at the end of my warm-up. You don't have to throw hard for a long time. Don't waste your energy. I took a breather while the managers and umpires exchanged line-up cards and went over the ground rules at home plate. There is generally another minute or two after the managers get back before your team takes the field.

The relief pitcher will help himself if he loosens up to the point where he is close to being ready the first time he gets up. From there on, he just throws easy to keep himself loose. Inexperienced pitchers will throw hard every time they get up. Save your energy for the game and don't tire yourself out in the bullpen.

To be a good relief pitcher takes considerable experience. At times you must get ready quickly, and sometimes you may get up and throw five or six times at different intervals. The reliever must develop a different approach to pitching from a starter's. He must go with his best right away. He doesn't have enough time to set up the hitter. He probably will face a hitter only once in a game. The reliever generally comes in with men on and can't afford to be cute and walk someone. Be extra careful with your first pitch when you appear in relief in a tough situation. The batter is swinging; concentrate on keeping the ball *down*.

Pitchers should be rested and not overworked, but I believe being strong is overemphasized. Working a lot is better than not pitching often enough!

6. Suggestions to Your Manager

If a manager uses the following procedure he can make it easy on the pitching staff.

He should notify each pitcher in advance who is starting, who is long man, and who is short man, so each will know how much and how hard to work out before the game.

He should give the signal early enough to give the reliever sufficient time to get ready. He should give a sign whether he wants him to go slow or get ready quickly. There is no need for the relief pitcher to be throwing fast and furious if the manager has already decided to go with the starting pitcher for a while and has no intention of taking him out. In the major leagues telephones are usually used, but if phones are not available or not used, the hat is usually used as a signal. If the manager looks down to the bullpen and takes off his hat, he wants to know if his relief pitcher is loose and ready to go in. If the catcher, pitcher, or pitching coach lifts his hat off his head, he is simply saying he's ready. If no hat is lifted, the manager may do something to stall till he sees the hat go up.

A manager may sometimes make the mistake of getting mad or losing patience with the pitcher on the mound, and he will then wave the relief pitcher in from the bullpen as soon as he leaves the dugout. This is poor managing. A manager should do the same thing every time, so his pitchers learn his mannerisms. For example, a slow walk to the mound means the pitcher is gone. This gives the reliever a chance to throw five or ten hard pitches from the time the manager leaves the dugout till he gets to the mound and makes his decision known to the umpire. A hustling gait or quick walk or jog by the manager usually means the pitcher is not coming out, and the reliever can take a breather or slow down and save himself.

A manager should realize that a pitcher who warms up three or four times quickly and hard has taken something out of himself and should be treated as if he had pitched in a game, even though he hasn't been used that day.

Through the years I have noticed that many managers waste their pitching by having two pitchers warm up at the same time during the early phase of the game. There are certainly some occasions when this is necessary, but there is usually little sense in wasting an arm. Naturally in the latter part of the game it is more likely that two pitchers will be up throwing at the same time, usually a left-hander and a right-hander.

In my estimation Al Lopez was the best defensive

manager that I played for and the best handler of a pitching staff. Everyone knew where he fitted into the staff, as starter, long man, or short man, and Lopez stayed with his program unless something unexpected occurred.

He also brought young pitchers along better than any manager I have seen. Paul Richards has also had much success with young pitchers. On many teams that I played for, a young pitcher brought up from the minors would be put in immediately to start. He would be extra nervous, have little or no knowledge of the hitters, and feel completely unsettled. The end results were generally poor; he lost confidence and either sat around or soon after was sent back to the minors. There is no reason to throw a young pitcher to the wolves and jeopardize his career by rushing him in as a starter.

Al would generally nurse the young pitcher along in long relief, each assignment more demanding, many times taking the pitcher out sooner than you would expect in order to build up his confidence—if he had pitched one more inning he might have gotten hit. When the starting assignment was finally awarded, it was selected against a team that would give the pitcher the best chance to win. Another beneficial move that Al used frequently was to bring back a pitcher the very next day after he had had a poor outing. This didn't allow the pitcher to brood and it showed the confidence the manager had in the pitcher. The results were usually most rewarding.

One of the main reasons the Los Angeles Dodgers have had such outstanding success is the way Walter Alston, the dean of managers, has handled his pitching staff through the years.

XIX / Bunting, Sliding, and Running

There are four outstanding baseball instructors from whom I learned most of the following fundamentals: Bernie DeViveiros, a scout in the Detroit chain for many years; Grover Resinger, who managed in the Cardinal organization for many years and more recently was third-base coach for the White Sox and Tigers; Cookie Lavagetto, who was an outstanding coach and instructor when I was with the San Francisco Giants; and Whitey Herzog, whose daily tutoring expedited the development of a number of New York Met ballplayers.

1. Bunting

As I mentioned in a previous chapter, it is wrong, in my opinion, to keep the bat level when you bunt, because the chances of a pop-up are greatly increased. A right-handed hitter should bunt with the right hand above and ahead of the left, making it almost impossible to pop the bunt up. Keep the bat from the start at the top of the strike zone. Any pitch above the bat would then be a ball.

The batter should not square around, for he would then give the play away in advance, allowing the infielders to come in quicker, and he would have to use

P-134A   P-134B

P-134C

too much foot, body, and head movement. Bend your knees to bunt the low ball.

With a runner on first, the ball is bunted to the first-base side. With a runner on second, the ball is bunted to the third-base side. I found that by reaching out a little bit I could bunt toward third more easily than if I pulled my left hand back to change the angle of the bat. Simply slide the right hand up to the label to bunt. The left hand moves up slightly. Do not grip the bat tightly. The hand at the label of the bat should hold the bat mostly with the index and middle fingers and the thumb. Don't wrap your hand around the bat (P-134A, B, C; C is not recommended unless you have trouble with B).

Move up in the batter's box. This will increase your chances of bunting a fair ball, and you will not bunt a ball that will hit home plate and bounce up to the catcher.

2. Sliding

There is only *one* correct way to slide, and that is with a bent leg. This way, you have no chance to break your leg. The leg that is broken is the lead leg. In the bent-leg slide, that leg is bent underneath with the spikes in a position where they cannot catch the ground. You can get to the bag faster with this slide. You do not get strawberries on your hips because you slide on the outside of the lower leg. You can do the up-and-run. You can see what you are doing, and you can do a variety of slides from the bent leg.

Never slide in a sandpit. The best sliding surface is grass. Practice with shoes off. Run as hard as you can. Bend your leg underneath and, as you slide, lean back. This will keep you from jamming the lead knee into the ground. After you are more experienced,

184

slide with the upper body in an upright position. Hands should not touch the ground unless you slide by the bag and have to reach for it. Hands should be at least head-high (P-135).

Put grass or dirt in your hands. This will force you to raise your hands, and you won't jam them down on the dirt when you slide and injure a hand or wrist.

A pitcher should slide straight in to all the bases. Don't hook-slide into home plate; go straight in. If you hook-slide into home plate and the catcher plants his foot in front of the plate, you will bounce off, not touching the plate.

P-135

3. Running

In baseball I never hear any instructions about the correct fundamentals of running. Pitchers run every day, and they might just as well run correctly.

Run with the toes straight ahead. As you can see in the picture, if you run with your toes out, you will lose 1½ inches. If you take 20 steps, you will lose more than 2 feet (P-136A, B). Run on the balls of the feet. Run with the body slightly forward

P-136A

P-136B

(P-137). Bring the knees straight up in front, not to the side (P-138A—correct; P-138B—incorrect). Reach out with your feet after you bring your knees up. Don't run as if you wanted to kick your rear end with your heels. Use your arms like pistons, or make believe you are pulling yourself along by pulling on an imaginary rope. Keep the elbows in (P-139).

4. The Delayed Steal

There are times when a pitcher with good speed can use the regular steal. The delayed steal can be used by a fast runner as well as by a runner with below-average speed. Probably a pitcher would want to use this play toward the end of the game in a situation where one run would decide the ball game.

The delayed steal by the pitcher is best used with two outs and a singles hitter at the plate. Remember, it would take two singles to score the pitcher from first.

The runner should observe where the second baseman and shortstop are playing. The chances for success are best when a straight-away hitter is at the plate and both infielders are playing him accordingly. If a right-handed pull hitter was up, the second baseman would be playing way over toward second base,

P-137

P-138A

P-138B

and the element of surprise in the delayed steal wouldn't work on him because he would be so close to the bag.

The runner takes his normal lead. When the pitcher starts to throw home, the runner takes three "bunny hops" with his body facing the pitcher—not turning his shoulders as if he were going to run to second. He tries to keep his body as low to the ground as possible, so as not to be conspicuous, and the bunny hops are done by reaching out with the right foot and then bringing the left foot to it. After he has done the three bunny hops, and no sooner, he turns and runs to second. This play is successful because the infielder who would be covering for an ordinary steal has looked home after watching the runner and seeing that his shoulders are not turned toward second. The catcher also does not see the runner break for second. The three bunny hops have taken the runner way off the bag; it is simply a race for second between the runner and the second base-man or shortstop. Sometimes the catcher throws the ball and no one is covering second. Also check to see if the shortstop and second baseman take a couple of steps toward second base after each pitch, which they should. If they don't, your chances are much better.

P-139

XX / Equipment and Care

P-140

1. Selecting a Glove

A great deal has been said about getting the biggest glove possible for a pitcher. Yet if you have a small hand, a big glove may not fit and may be most uncomfortable. I recommend getting the size glove that fits your hand.

A full web helps prevent anyone from seeing into the glove (P-140).

It is a mistake to put just any oil on a glove. Oil will make the glove heavy, and some oil will get on your fingers and prevent you from getting the proper grip. The glove-manufacturing companies have come up with a glove-conditioner that helps the leather breathe, conditions it, and yet has no oily feel to it. I recommend this.

The first thing you should do when you get a new glove is put it in water. Then put it on your hand and hit it with your fist to form it to your hand. The water brings the fibers of the padding together so that your glove, as it gets older, doesn't have a tendency to get floppy. The wet glove will mold to the hand much faster than it would if you did not wet it.

188

2. Shoes

Try not to skimp on your shoes. Buy a good pair and remember they should fit snugly. If they are too big, your left foot will slip inside the shoe when the left foot makes contact with the ground. This slight give is enough to affect your control.

A leather toe plate is the best. It should be put on at the factory.

3. Hat

Always wear your hat when you pitch. When you pitch in a game, you must wear a hat, so practice with one on.

4. Sweatshirt

Always have your arm covered. The temperature is not the major enemy of the pitcher. The thing to guard against is the wind. It will lower your body temperature too fast. The fellow with bulging muscles may like to let his girl friend see them, but if you're smart, take care of that arm, keep it covered. You can always get another girl friend, but you cannot get another arm. Wool is the best material for a sweatshirt, as it absorbs the sweat.

5. Supporter and Cup

Almost all players in professional baseball use a supporter and cup to protect themselves from injury while playing.

6. Sanitary Stockings

Many ball players use rubber bands to hold up their stockings, but these have a tendency to reduce circu-

P-141A

P-141D

P-141B

P-141E

P-141C

P-141F

P-141G

P-141H

P-141I

lation in the legs. Using adhesive tape is inconvenient, and the tape is hard to get off. When you put on your stockings, pull the sanitary sock all the way up. Then pull the stocking all the way up. Roll the stocking over twice and pull the sanitary sock down over it. Turn both together over once. Twist the sanitary sock till it is tight, and tuck the end under the roll. Your stockings will not fall down (P-141A–I).

7. Care of the Arm

The most important piece of equipment you have is your arm. Take care of it accordingly.

Always remember when you work hard and use your muscles, in the beginning stiffness and soreness cannot be avoided. These are typical problems for all pitchers. Continue your daily routine, and after three or four days the stiffness and soreness should be gone. After you pitch in a ball game, use *no heat*. If you treat the arm and shoulder, use ice for at least twenty minutes. Many major-league pitchers use ice after they pitch. Sandy Koufax and Don Drysdale of the Los Angeles Dodgers made the ice treatment popular. The picture of Bill Singer, of the Los Angeles Dodgers, taken July 20, 1970, after he pitched a no-hitter, shows him soaking his arm in

P-142

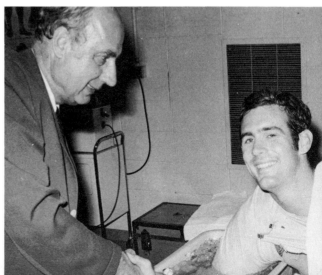

ice, with team physician Dr. Robert Woods congratulating him (P-142). Ice in plastic bags is held in place by an ace bandage; the elbow is submerged in ice.

There is always a certain amount of capillary bleeding, which causes stiffness and soreness. The ice treatment reduces this, speeds the recovery, and greatly reduces stiffness.

Twenty-four hours after you pitch, you may use heat to reduce stiffness and soreness. One of the best treatments is the whirlpool bath. If it is not available, put a towel over the shoulder and run water, as hot as you can stand it, over the shoulder and arm. Heating pads and heat lamps are also very helpful.

Always follow the advice of your club physician or trainer.

When you warm up, by all means start easy. Don't be a fool and try to impress by showing off too quickly. It only takes one severe injury to bring your search for the pot of gold to a screeching halt.

Suggestions: Don't ride with the pitching arm out the window of a car. If there is a great deal of wind, wear a windbreaker when you are standing around. Don't stand around with a wet undershirt; change it and come back out. Don't throw anything but a baseball. Bring a sweater or jacket to night games and when it is cool, so you can put it on after the game.

XXI / Recovery from Injury

Even though you may throw correctly, there is still always the possibility of arm injury. During the sixteen years that I pitched professionally, I had two serious injuries. The first occurred in my third year of baseball and happened in the twelfth inning of a 1–1 ball game. I tore the tendon in my elbow on a curve ball. The orthopedic specialist in Montgomery, Alabama, told me, even though I had torn the tendon away from the bone, to keep throwing easy, not to immobilize the arm. Complete immobilization would cause extra scar tissue to the point where I would never regain normal use. He also told me that it would take at least three months before I would be able to pitch in a ballgame.

"Throwing easy" may at first be mere lobbing of the ball from as close as fifteen feet. If you have a severe injury, heat of all kinds is beneficial. Massage is beneficial. Keep running. You have a long recovery period ahead of you, but if you don't give up and can endure some pain, you almost certainly will make it back.

My second injury occurred in the major leagues a day and a half after I had pitched eight and two-thirds innings. After throwing five pitches in the bullpen, I was called in to pitch in relief. After the seven warm-up pitches, my first pitch resulted in a torn shoulder muscle.

Both of these injuries could have been avoided if the manager had used better judgment. In the first case, a young pitcher should not be allowed to over-extend himself to the point where fatigue has set in. In the second case the manager had forgotten that a day and a half before I had pitched an almost complete ball game, that it was cold, and that he had not given me ample time to warm up. The result could have been the end of a career. At the same time that I hurt my shoulder, Vernon Law and Frank Lary unfortunately suffered the same serious injury. Frank Lary came back a year or two later but was never the same. Vernon Law took almost two years to recover. I know that Vernon followed a very rigid exercise program, and this is the reason he did eventually come back. As for myself, I went to Florida that winter and followed a daily program of strengthening and flexibility exercises plus running, swimming, and throwing. I am sure that it was because of this tremendous exercise program that I was able to come back the following year and produce.

For anyone sustaining an injury, I recommend seeing an orthopedic specialist and following his advice. But be ready to start on a long, hard work program of exercise, flexibility, and throwing to guarantee your return to the mound, and be ready to endure a considerable amount of pain.

The exercises recommended in Chapter X are ideal for a pitcher recovering from an arm injury.

XXII / Diet and the Athlete

For your sake, don't turn away from this chapter. Diet is as essential to good pitching as is the downward plane. The proper diet for an athlete is the key to withstanding the rigors of baseball. You must eat properly to fuel up the body's motor for high speed, long distances, and rough roads.

I see many baseball men grab a hot dog, gulp down a cola beverage, relish a piece of pie, doughnut, or coffee roll, and then charge onto the field for a game. The fuel they put into their body machines is of low octane, has a lot of impurities, and is overprocessed. It will give poor mileage and no pick-up, and may ruin the motor.

The athlete must take a good look at his diet to make sure he is not going to be one of the millions of people who develop coronary thrombosis, hardening of the arteries, cancer, arthritis, and other degenerative diseases. The athlete must know that processing, added chemicals, and poor soil produce inferior food. Inferior food produces inferior people. If you don't eat properly, you also risk the chance of being away from the ball park because of illness—colds, sore throats, stomach disorders, and so on.

What should the athlete know about diet and nutrition? What foods should he eat? What foods should he avoid?

Vitamins are not stored in the body. You need them every day. Heat destroys most vitamins. For example, canned foods have been heated at the canning plant; you heat them again, and leftovers may be heated a third time. The result: little nutritional value. Professional ballplayers travel a great deal by plane, where food is heated in advance and kept hot for a long time. In essence, the nutritional value is hardly enough to maintain the physical well-being of an athlete.

Most modern foods are processed, and much of the nutritional value is lost. The product is high in calories but low in nutrition.

Eat three meals a day. Don't skip breakfast.

1. Breakfast

Drink juice (orange, grapefruit, tomato, prune, pineapple, papaya) or eat fresh fruit (figs, melon, strawberries, peaches, prunes, bananas, blueberries).

For hot cereal, eat cream of wheat or oatmeal and use honey as a sweetener, not sugar. The cold cereals of today have little value, but if you go for Rice Krispies or cornflakes, be sure to eat them with fresh fruits (bananas, strawberries, blueberries, fresh peaches) and with honey as sweetener.

Boiled or poached eggs are better for you than fried eggs. You may include meat—ham, bacon, or sausage.

Whole-wheat toast is recommended over white toast. I think honey is better for you than jam or jelly. Buckwheat and whole-wheat pancakes are better than white-flour pancakes.

The athlete should eliminate coffee from his diet.

Skim milk is recommended; try to reduce the amount of fat you consume.

Avoid the breakfast that consists of coffee and a

roll or pastry or a piece of white toast and jelly. This is a poor diet for an athlete to start a day on.

2. Lunch

Salads are good—tuna fish or other fish, egg, and so on.

Soups—home made, if possible (lentil, split pea, bean, onion, marrow-bone, vegetable, broths, clam chowder)—are all good for you.

Eat fresh fruit.

Drink skim milk, fresh juice, or iced tea.

Ask for whole-wheat rather than white bread when you have sandwiches.

3. Dinner

Drink fruit juice. Try to eliminate cola drinks.

Homemade soups are preferable.

Appetizers may include chopped chicken livers, marinated herring, shrimp or crabmeat cocktail, to name a few.

Once a week, eat organ meat such as sweetbreads, liver, kidneys, heart, or brains. These contain tremendous amounts of vitamins and minerals.

Twice a week, eat fish or seafood. Once a week, eat poultry—chicken, turkey, or duck. Fill in the rest of the week with beef, lamb, pork, or veal.

Fresh vegetables are better for you than frozen ones, and frozen are better than canned vegetables.

Eat baked potatoes, yams, or sweet potatoes with their skins on. Try to eliminate french-fried potatoes from your diet.

Salads of all kinds are good for you and should be part of your dinner—all kinds of lettuce, onions, avocado, radishes, cucumbers, tomatoes, celery, pepper, watercress, fruit, carrots, and cabbage.

Dessert may be any kind of fruit; for example, figs,

raisins, apricots, apples. All kinds of nuts are nutritious. Natural cheeses are far superior to pastry and pies.

Try to eliminate or greatly reduce your consumption of candy and ice cream. These items are high in sugar and reduce your appetite. If the little bit you eat besides these items is not high in nutritional value, you are putting a tremendous burden on your body by expecting it to function without supplying it with the nutritional materials to help it run properly.

Alcoholic beverages should be eliminated or limited to mealtime.

All condiments should be avoided or used in moderation.

Stay away from gravies and greasy foods.

Because much food is not as good as it should be, because of the processing and chemicals used, and because of the type of diet that is prevalent in America, and because athletes eat out a great deal, a food supplement is highly recommended. *I suggest you talk to your personal physician and ask him to recommend a vitamin-mineral supplement for you to take; or use the vitamin-mineral supplement provided by the ball club.* Some people may call you a "health nut." But remember, without good health your life can be one big dark cloud. Good health is your most prized possession.

One more thing: *do not smoke.*

XXIII / Ingredients You Must Have to Be a Success

Harry Walker, an excellent hitting coach, now a manager, many years ago gave me this list of ingredients necessary for success:

1. *Attitude*—an attitude to become the best.
2. *Initiative*—you can talk about it, but you must have the initiative to do it.
3. *Thoroughness*—the ability to stick to it and work until you have improved or accomplished what you set out to do.
4. *Concentration*—the ability to concentrate on one specific objective; don't let your mind wander.
5. *Observation*—some people have their eyes open but see nothing; observe and decipher the bad from the good.
6. *Creative imagination*—the ability to think for oneself.
7. *Decision*—have the ability to assume the responsibility of your own decisions.
8. *Adaptability*—the ability to adjust quickly to different situations and events.
9. *Leadership*—a rare ability which manifests itself in many forms.
10. *Organizing*—the ability to plan your time and daily activities in a way to achieve your specific goals.
11. *Expression*—the ability to convey thoughts to others.

12. *Knowledge*—there is no substitute for proper use of knowledge.

You now have to ask yourself: Am I ready to pay the price to become one of the greats and collect the pot of gold at the end of the rainbow?

Afterword

I don't care how good or bad your pitching is at present. If you can continue to improve, eventually you will reach the top. For some it may be a twenty-four-hour job. The road you must travel is long and set with traps. You must follow the rules for success:

Use proper body mechanics
Do strengthening and flexibility exercises daily
Learn to concentrate and relax
Know the weaknesses of the batters
Develop the proper mental attitude
Eat a proper diet
Have the will to win and don't discourage easily
Practice, practice, practice

Please do not cite exceptions to defend your failure to follow these rules. I think you will be doing an injustice to yourself and your baseball future.

This book does not answer all the questions, I am sure, but I sincerely hope it will bring to the forefront the importance of mechanics. I hope more books will be written on the same subject, so that more pitchers will be able to reach the pot of gold at the end of the rainbow.

Stop reading, and get to work. I'll see you in the big leagues.

Best of luck,
BOB SHAW

Index

A

Adams, Red, 37, 53
alcoholic beverages, 198
Alston, Walter, 182
arching, 49, 51
arms
  care of, 177, 189, 191–92
    exercises for, 124, 140
  injuries to, 193–94
  position and motion of,
    27, 36
    arm-hooking, 34, 37, 42, 55
    change-up pitch, 97
    for hitter, 165
    lead arm, 17, 41–42, 56
    short arm vs. long arm,
      54–55
    slider, 94
    throwing arm, 10, 12,
      36–38, 42–43, 45–46,
      47, 49, 51, 52, 53,
      54–55, 57, 105–106
    windup, 33

B

balk, 143, 147, 174
ball
  breaking, 13, 14, 85, 86, 88,
    89, 92, 94, 98
  damage to, 100
  hiding of, 33
  spin, 81, 82, 83, 86, 89, 91,
    93, 94, 96, 97, 98, 99,
    107
  see also grip, on ball
bases
  backing up, 155–57
  running, 185–86
  sliding, 184–85
  stealing, 29, 142, 143
    defense against, 29,
      142–43, 147
    delayed steal, 186–87
    see also pick-off plays
batter, *see* hitter
beanball, 116
Bernoulli's principle, 43, 83
Berres, Ray, 4, 5
beverages, 141, 196–98
Blackwell, Ewell, 10
body, upper, position and
    motion of, 17, 19, 45, 46,
    49, 51, 52, 55, 56, 57
  see also shoulders, position
    and motion of
breaking ball, *see* ball, breaking
breaking hands, *see* hands,
    position and motion of,
    breaking
Brewer, Jim, 24
broom handle (as teaching aid),
    105–106

Buhl, Bob, 8
bullpen, 177
bunting, 183–84
    fielding against, 153–55
    pitching in bunt situation,
        174–75
Burdette, Lew, 171

C

Campanis, Al: on learning
        problems, 103–104
catcher, 27, 163
catcher and pitcher, relationship,
        158–62, 178
    signals, 142, 143, 152, 155,
        158–61, 162, 179
change-up pitch, 96–97,
        140–41, 179
clothing, *see* equipment and
        clothing
collapsing, 49, 51
control, 4, 5, 13–16, 81
curve ball, 8, 12, 13, 14, 23, 45,
        47, 51, 80, 85, 86, 88–91,
        94, 100, 140–41, 179
    slow curve, 96
    see also slider (fast curve ball)

D

Davis, Tommy, 14
delivery, *see* overhand delivery;
        sidearm delivery; three-
        quarter-arm delivery
DeViveiros, Bernie, 183
diet, 122, 195–98
dipping, 49, 51
double play, covering for,
        144–45
downward plane, pitching on,
        8–14, 16–55
Drysdale, Don, 10, 191

E

elbow
    exercises for, 124
    injuries to, 39, 90, 94
    position and motion of, 10,
        12, 29, 33, 34, 35, 36,
        41, 42, 47, 49, 52, 55,
        57, 81, 86, 89, 93, 98
    for hitter, 166
equipment and clothing, 141,
        177, 189, 191
Erskine, Carl, 97
exercises, 120–24, 130, 132,
        137, 139–41, 175–76, 194

F

fast ball, 8, 13, 14, 27, 45, 80,
        82, 84–85, 93, 94, 140–41,
        169, 170, 172, 173, 174,
        175, 179
    see also sinker; slider (fast
        curve ball)
feet
    care of, 189
    position and motion of
        follow-through, 51
        for hitter, 165
        lead foot, 26, 31, 33, 34,
            47, 49, 51
        pivot foot, 19, 21–24, 26,
            33, 47, 49, 51, 56, 97
        running, 185–86
        stance, 16–17, 19
        stride, 47
        windup, 31, 33
Feller, Bob, 35
fielding plays, 110, 153–57
    double plays, 144–45
follow-through, 19, 41–42, 43,
        46, 51–52, 55, 57, 107
Ford, Whitey, 176–77
fork ball, 99

G

glove, 188
grip
  on ball, 80–82, 84, 86, 88,
    91, 92–93, 93–94, 96,
    97, 98, 100
  across the seams, 81–82,
    84, 86, 93
  horseshoe grip, 86
  Maglie grip, 86
  with the seams, 81, 82,
    84, 86, 93
  on bat, 81

H

hands
  exercises for, 130
  position and motion of, 55,
    56, 57
  breaking, 29, 31, 37–38,
    42, 51, 53, 56, 81
  curve ball, 90
  fielding plays, 153
  glove hand, 17, 33, 41, 42,
    94
  hiding the ball, 33
  for hitter, 14, 166
  pick-off plays, 146
  set position, 29
  slider, 94
  in sliding, 185
  slip pitch, 98
  stance, 17
  throwing hand, 17, 33, 38,
    41, 43, 45–46, 47, 90, 98
  windup, 31, 33
  see also grip, on ball
head
  exercises for, 124
  position of, 17, 31, 45, 52–53,
    109

health, *see* diet; exercises;
    smoking
Herzog, Whitey, 183
hiding the ball, 33
hiding the pitch, 31
high pitch, 14, 27, 29, 36, 38,
    82, 117, 166, 171
hips, position and motion of,
    19, 23–24, 33–34, 35, 46,
    56, 57
hitter, 8, 14, 23, 41
  arms, 165
  bunting, 174–75, 183–84
  curve ball, 8, 14, 167
  elbow, 166
  feet, 165
  getting hit by the ball, 116
  grip, 81
  hands, 14, 166
  high ball vs. low ball, 14, 166
  left-handed hitter, 23, 94, 98,
    166
  relationship to pitcher, 116–
    119
  jamming the hitter, 94, 165
    pitcher's mental attitude
      toward, 112, 114, 116–
      117
    pitcher's observations and
      notes, 100–11, 164–68
  right-handed hitter, 23, 98
  stance, 164–65
  wrists, 167
Holt, Goldie, 108

I

inside pitch, 24, 26, 27, 117,
    118, 167, 170, 171

K

Kaline, Al, 117
knuckle ball, 98–99
Koufax, Sandy, 12, 191

L

Lary, Frank, 194
Lavagetto, Cookie, 183
Law, Vernon, 194
legs
  care of, 189, 191
  injuries to, 184
  position and motion of, 51
    back leg, 12, 29, 37, 38,
      46, 49, 51–52, 57, 96
    change-up pitch, 96
    follow-through and after,
      51–52, 54
    kick, 19, 34, 35, 37, 42, 56
    lead leg, 27, 29, 34–36, 37,
      42, 46, 51, 54, 55, 56,
      57, 81
    set position, 27, 29
    sliding, 184
    stance, 19, 56
    stride, 46
    windup, 31
long arm, 54–55
"long man," 176
Lopat, Ed, 141
Lopez, Al, 181–82
low pitch, 14, 27, 117, 166,
  167, 171, 174

M

Maltz, Maxwell: *Psycho-
  Cybernetics,* 119
Marichal, Juan, 12, 19, 24, 35,
  56, 85, 161
Martin, Freddie, 85
mental aspects, 5–6, 102, 104,
  109–15, 199–200
  aggressiveness and
    competitive spirit, 113,
    117, 119
  concentration, 109–10, 119,
    172, 199

confidence, 111–13, 114, 170
emotional stability, 104, 113–
  114, 163
memory, development of,
  110–11
pitcher and hitter, relationship, 112, 114, 116–17
pitcher and umpire, relationship, 163
relaxation, 111, 112, 172
Meyers, Kenny, 46
mirror (as teaching aid), 106
missing the plate, 26–27
motion pictures (as teaching
  aid), 106–107
mudball, 100

N

"nickel curve," *see* slider (fast
  curve ball)

O

Oliva, Tony, 14
outside pitch, 24, 26, 27, 117,
  118, 167, 170, 171, 174
overhand delivery, 13
  change-up pitch, 96–97
  curve ball, 13, 86
  fast ball, 13, 84
  grip, 82
  hands, breaking, 38
  leg kick, 19, 35
  stance, 27, 29

P

palm ball, 97
Pascual, Camilo, 38, 46
pepper, 42, 175, 176
Pierce, Billy, 45
pick-off plays, 24, 142–43,
  146–52

first base, 24, 146–47, 151–
152
first base and second base,
148–49
by left-handed pitcher, 24,
149, 150, 151–52
second base, 149–50, 152,
155
signals, 148–49, 152, 155
third base, 150, 151–52
Podres, Johnny, 97
pop-ups, back up for, 157

Q

quick pitch, 173–74

R

reflexes, 42
relief pitcher, 176, 179–81, 182
Resinger, Grove, 183
Richards, Paul, 97–98, 182
Rickey, Branch, 21
Rose, Pete, 14
rosin bag, 141
rubber, 17, 19, 21–24, 26, 37, 56,
143
running, 185–86
rushing, 19, 29, 31, 33, 34, 36–
37, 52, 53–54, 55

S

Sain, Johnny, 88, 89, 93, 107,
176
screwball, 24, 98
set position, 53
hands, 29
with men on base, 52, 143,
172
warm up, 179
Shaw, John H.: exercise
program, 123

Shellenback, Frank, 99
short arm, 54–55
"short man," 176
shoulders
exercises for, 124
injuries to, 34, 55
position and motion of,
27, 55, 56
back shoulder, 10, 35, 46
lead shoulder, 10, 33–34,
35, 38, 41, 42, 46, 47,
49, 53, 98
sidearm delivery, 8, 10, 13
Singer, Bill, 91–92
sinker, 80, 82, 84–85
slider (fast curve ball), 13, 80,
85, 92–94, 96, 174, 179
sliding, 184–85
slip pitch, 97–98
slurve (pitch between slider and
curve), 94
smoking, 198
Spahn, Warren, 4, 19, 35, 151
spitball, 99–100
stance, 16–17, 19, 31, 56
closed, 27
of hitter, 164–65
open, 27
square, 27, 29, 54, 56
stealing bases, *see* bases, stealing
stopwatch (as teaching aid),
108
strategy, 118, 143, 169–82
stride, 52, 46–47, 57
swimming (as exercise), 137,
139

T

target, importance of, 31, 106,
109, 118–19, 162, 179
teaching aids, 103, 105–108
figure eight, 47, 49, 105
teaching methods, 101–104

Index

tempo, 16, 53–54
three-quarter-arm delivery,
    13, 38
  change-up pitch, 96
  curve ball, 13, 86
  fast ball, 13
  grip, 82
  hands, breaking, 38
  leg kick, 35
  pick-off plays, 147
  slider, 13
  stance, 27, 29

U

umpire and pitcher, relationship,
    163

W

walk, intentional, 162
Walker, Harry, 199–200

warm up, 177–80, 192
water, drinking, 141
wild pitch, 27
  back up for, 157
Wilhelm, Hoyt, 99
Williams, Ted, 117
Wills, Maury, 14, 151
windup, 31, 33
Woods, Dr. Robert, 192
wrist
  exercises for, 130
  injuries to, 90
  motion, 38, 57
    change-up pitch, 97
    curve ball, 47, 86, 88, 89,
      90
    fast ball, 85
    for hitter, 167
    slider, 92, 93
    slip pitch, none in, 97, 98
Wyatt, Whitlow, 92
Wynn, Early, 4, 141

4-2